Praise fo

No More Ba

"For those of you who have lost deeply, and for the rest of you who are in the batter's box, this book is for you. It's not pretty. It's not for the faint of heart. But I dare you to read along, as Gary unveils his MIRACLE story, not of how God restored what he once had, but how God re-storied Gary's new, beautiful path."

—**MARK STUART,** two-time Grammy award-winning lead singer of Audio Adrenaline and someone who also lost everything

"*No More Bad Days* is a rare gift for all of us. Gary tells a story full of more astonishing miracles than most small towns will have in a person's lifetime. That can be intimidating to read. So Gary chose to write with a self-effacing honesty that makes you want the book to never end. It's beautiful, redemptive, funny, instructive, vulnerable, and kind. He isn't just telling his story; he's offering a way of seeing life. Gary has learned the reality of 'Christ in Me,' and it has changed everything. I'm so honored to call him my friend. Enjoy."

—**JOHN LYNCH,** author of *On My Worst Day* and coauthor of *The Cure*

No More Bad Days

Foreword by Bart Millard of MercyMe

No More Bad Days

Trading the Pursuit of Perfection for the Gift of Grace

Gary Miracle
with Robert Noland

SALEM
BOOKS
an imprint of Regnery Publishing
Washington, D.C.

Cataloging-in-Publication data on file with the Library of Congress.

ISBN: 978-1-68451-419-9
eISBN: 978-1-68451-475-5

Published in the United States by
Salem Books
An Imprint of Regnery Publishing
A Division of Salem Media Group
Washington, D.C.
www.SalemBooks.com

Published in association with the literary agency of WTA Media, LLC., Franklin, Tennessee

Manufactured in the United States of America

10 9 8 7 6 5 4 3 2 1

This book is dedicated to

anyone who's ever had a bad day

CONTENTS

Take every thought
captive to obey Christ.

2 Corinthians 10:5 ESV

Foreword

by Bart Millard

The employment? Temporary. The friendship? Permanent.

My bandmates and I first met Gary twenty-plus years ago when he was working for Shepherd Ministries. MercyMe was leading worship at the weekend student conferences. As we got to know the staff, we quickly hit it off with Gary. That same year, we signed our record deal and decided to bring on our first employee outside the band. We needed a merch guy to travel with us, set up, and run the table with our CDs and T-shirts at every show. When you're living in tight quarters on a bus and hanging out twenty-four hours a day for weeks at a time, trust me, you want to be with people you actually like. Looking at our short list of possibilities, we called Gary and he accepted.

Over the years, we have joked that he was terrible at the job, mostly because he gave away too much stuff. But just a few months after "I Can Only Imagine" was released and blew up, we had to figure out a way to navigate all the changes coming at us. That was when we had a heart-to-heart with Gary and mutually decided to part ways. While the employment didn't last very long, we've remained close friends ever since.

When Gary was working at a car dealership or for Autotrader or whatever he might be selling at the time, occasionally he would call me and ask, "Hey, these people are fans of yours. Prove to them that I know you. Send me a picture or video." And I would do it. Sometimes, the whole band would get in on it. But there were random times here and there when I wouldn't respond, just so he would look foolish. (I had to keep the joke on him every once in a while to make sure he didn't get cocky.) But seriously, when you have done what we do for so long, you find out there are a handful of people you can call your true friends. Because we've known Gary virtually for the life of the band, he is definitely inside that tight circle.

Well before Gary got sick, he and I started discussing God's grace and identity in Christ. For several years, I had been working through these topics with people like John Lynch and Rusty Kennedy. When I began to share with Gary what I was learning, I remember him asking me, "Wait a minute . . . you're telling me that even on my worst day, Jesus is still in love with me?!"

Like me, Gary had grown up with a lot of legalism mixed in with faith. From there, we started having ongoing discussions, talking about what the New Testament teaches and what Jesus has done for us. I could tell it was turning Gary's world upside down. Of course, there was no way either of us could realize that was all part of God preparing him for what he was about to go through. Because I'm telling you, to live through anything like he has, to deal with that level of heartbreak, pain, and suffering, and to not have a grasp on who you are in Christ will mess you up. It will dismantle you fast.

When Gary got sick, we didn't know if he was going to make it, and that hit us all really hard. Then, when COVID hit, we were forced to watch his recovery from a distance. At the time, I was in the middle of writing a song called "Say I Won't." The lyrics had originally started out talking about where I was in my faith—embracing our identity in Christ and God's grace. (You can hear it in the first verse with lines like "driving thirty-five with a rocket inside, didn't know what I had" about the realization of understanding who we are in Jesus.) What is interesting is that Gary was even a part of that early version of the song because that's when we were having those ongoing discussions about grace.

After watching Gary literally fight for his life, finding out his limbs were going to have to be amputated, but seeing that he was going to make it, "Say I Won't" took a turn for me and became my personal outlet to write about what I was feeling while watching his journey. The song turned into an anthem of how life is so precious that we need to fight for it, changing to more of an overcomer song. Gary's battle to live became my inspiration for the chorus, the bridge, and the ending.

When the song was done, it felt like a natural move to make a music video. The record label wanted us to find some kind of hero story as the theme. They were throwing out different ideas, but they all involved people that we didn't know at all. While there was nothing wrong with that, it just felt inauthentic to us, like we were trying to sell something. I really wanted it to be someone we were personally invested in. So naturally, I asked, "What about Gary Miracle's story?"

When we approached Gary about being in the video, he answered, "I've been praying that God would use my story in a huge way, so everything that I've gone through wouldn't be in vain." Now, "Say I Won't" will forever connect Gary to us as a way to reach people with the Gospel.

No More Bad Days is a testament to the amazing number of folks we have seen find inspiration through Gary's story—people from all walks of life that he has been able to cross paths with and to whom he has given hope. It's been overwhelming, to say the least, that his testimony—shared with thousands on stages all over the country, and now through this book—started with him being in our video. That is worth everything to us.

Like Gary says, we all have bad days, and we all have hard times; what's important is what we choose to do next. Those are very real feelings with anything we are walking through in this life. When you understand what Gary has gone through and you witness his outlook on life, the bad things around you begin to shrink quickly.

I'm proud to call Gary Miracle my dear friend. I'm honored that he would ask me to speak to you in this foreword. *No More Bad Days* is his amazing story of healing and redemption. Seeing the beauty that's come out of the ashes of his life has been incredible, humbling, and inspiring to watch. I can't wait to see and hear about all the people who will be impacted by his story for the Kingdom of God.

INTRODUCTION

So, Is God Good?

At 7:18 a.m. on January 1, 2020, I died.

Starting on December 26 to that moment, in only a week, a virus reduced me from a healthy, six-foot-two, 240-pound, thirty-nine-year-old to flatlining in the intensive care unit of a Florida hospital.

By late April, I had become a quadruple amputee—losing most of all four of my limbs due to an extended period on life support that caused poor blood and oxygen supply to them.

Yet, since then, God has taken me from a divorced father of four struggling with the difficulties of life as an amputee to a remarried father of seven who now travels the nation encouraging others through my story. There have been plenty of other miracles since I was brought back to life that I want to tell you about in the pages ahead.

When I meet people, here's the most frequently asked question: "Is 'Miracle' really your last name?" The answer is yes, that is my actual name. But my life finally caught up to my name in 2020 when God gave new meaning through His work in me—the kind He has done throughout history that transforms Abrams into Abrahams, Sarais into Sarahs, and Sauls into Pauls. My name has always been Miracle, but now I am a miracle. God didn't have to change my name when He chose to change my life.

While my life was saved, losing my limbs proved that the end result isn't always what we expect. Because of my situation, I have come to realize that the best way to look at life's circumstances is through the lens of eternity. The only way that choice is even possible is with our Heavenly Father, the only One who can offer true hope and redemption. That's why for me, the real story you'll read in this book is not about *what* happened to me, but *Who* happened to me.

While I was lying in a hospital bed fighting for my life, my family had to decide to show the world that we believe God is good. When I realized my life would be affected forever, I decided to show the world that I believe He is good, too. When so many people have looked at me and wondered how I could go on, my only answer has been, "How could I *not*?"

My purpose in these pages is not just to tell you about the miracle that happened to me, but to show you that you are a miracle, too. This book may be about my journey, but it's written to you and for you. Regardless of your circumstances, I want you to connect with and relate to the battles I have fought and must fight every day—the first being to choose to believe that God wants to do something big, real, and amazing in you, just as He has done in me. But to accept His offer, you'll have to first see life through His lens and realize that, while you may be in a tough place, you can live with the mindset of "no more bad days."

While I certainly didn't lose as much as the Bible tells us Job did, I do understand experiencing a life-altering tragedy and questioning God's plan through the trauma and the drama. After all the dialogue with his "friends" and the monologue from God, Job comes to a powerful personal conclusion about his crisis:

> Then Job replied to the LORD:
> "I know that you can do anything, and no one can stop you. You asked, 'Who is this that questions my wisdom with such ignorance?' It is I—and I was talking about things I knew nothing about, things far too wonderful for me. You said, 'Listen and I will speak! I have some questions for you, and you must answer them.' I had only heard about you before, but now I have seen you with my own eyes." (Job 42:1–5)

Wherever you are right now—mentally, emotionally, or spiritually—and whatever has or hasn't happened to you, I want to invite you to walk with me through this story. I want to share how I was brought to a place of brokenness and humility to confess, "Lord, I had only heard about you before, but now I have seen You with my own eyes."

I pray that by the end of this book, you see God as good. Because He is.

I hope you see Him with your own eyes. And you can.

CHAPTER ONE

Working for Affirmation, Praying for Approval

I was born in Pontiac, Michigan, on July 15, 1981. All my extended family still live there—grandparents, aunts, uncles, everyone. We go there to visit them as often as we can.

In 1991, when I was ten years old, my dad's employer, Sea Ray Boats, promoted him and we moved to Merritt Island, Florida. To this day, I still live in the Sunshine State. And I'm blessed to be able to say my parents are still happily married. I have one sister, Jennifer, who's four years older than me. Throughout my life, we have been a close family foursome.

About a month after we left Michigan, my mom struck up a conversation with a lady at a laundromat who invited our family to her church in Rockledge, a nearby community. The next Sunday, Mom took Jennifer and me with her. Dad didn't go. Sunday was always the day he cut the grass. But after a few weeks of seeing that we were committed to going, he decided to change his yard day and join us. Dad never missed another Sunday after that.

Mom's father was a pastor, so she grew up as a "preacher's kid," but Dad had a different background. In fact, when he proposed to my mother the first time, she said no because he wasn't a Christian. But over time, as their love grew, she finally said yes. When Dad started going to church with us, he heard the Gospel, understood it for the first time, and became a committed follower of Christ. From that point forward, my parents were always on the same page and their strong spiritual alliance consistently influenced how our family approached life.

Eventually, Dad began volunteering in the youth department. Around the time I entered middle school, he became the church's part-time youth pastor while still working full-time for Sea Ray. My sister also made a decision to follow Christ after we started going to the church in Rockledge.

And my time came on October 6, 1991, at a Sunday night service. I can still picture exactly where I was sitting. Pastor Randy was leading the church in what was known as a "call to worship." He offered some inspiring one-liners, inviting and encouraging people into celebration and praise with the worship team.

I remember standing up with the congregation, listening intently, and then praying the kind of prayer I had heard so many times during that season of life. "Dear Jesus, please forgive me for my sins and come into my heart. I want to go to Heaven to be with You one day." Short, simple, and straightforward.

After my prayer, I remember feeling a distinct sense of pride about my decision. I couldn't wait for the church service to end so I could tell Mom and Dad. A strong sense of peace came over me, like a weight had been lifted off my shoulders. *What weight does a ten-year-old have?* you ask. I'm not sure, but I just knew in that moment I felt very different. I felt lighter. Everything about the Gospel made sense to me as the truth came together in my heart and connected for the first time. That night, I knew I wanted to follow Christ for the rest of my life.

When we got home from church, I immediately told my family about my experience. I knew they would be glad to hear that, now, all four of us had made decisions for Christ. I later wrote out all my thoughts in my journal. I still have a picture of the page from that night—a cherished memento of the turning point in my faith. I'm grateful I can remember the date and all the details about that night, because that knowledge helped me later, when I would come to question my faith. From that point on, I became heavily involved in our church, never missing Wednesday nights when I was in a program called Kids for Christ.

While I wanted to grow in my newfound faith, I always struggled—to an unhealthy point—with being a people-pleaser. Church just gave me another place to add to my list. I started to learn how to be a different person on Sunday mornings, which is an area where I see so many people struggle.

I always craved approval and needed constant affirmation. I preferred getting both at the same time, if at all possible. That led me to become a chameleon as I was growing up, meaning whatever group I was in at the time and whoever I was with determined how I acted. I worked hard to be "all things to all people"—which is not only exhausting, but impossible.

By the time I entered high school, I had no problem setting my faith aside to join in whatever everyone else was doing. When I was at church, particularly after being promoted into the youth group, I tried to look like the perfect Christian. As the leader's son, I knew there was an expectation to live up to, so if I couldn't stand out to get affirmation, I at least wanted to blend in for approval. Trapped in a tug-of-war, I learned how to wear different masks to get by. I had a chronic identity crisis.

In elementary school, I got into sports, playing basketball and football. In middle school, I started running to get in better shape for basketball and discovered that I loved it. By my sophomore year in high school, I had decided to focus solely on track. I enjoyed the camaraderie with the other guys on the team while also being able to compete as an individual. That combination satisfied all my goals. I discovered I didn't have to try as hard as I did in other sports; I just naturally picked up running and was good at it. And, of course, there were plenty of accolades that came with winning.

In 1999 and 2000, my 4x800 relay team won back-to-back state championships. For two years, we never lost a race. I alternated between first leg and third leg, depending on where the coach wanted me. He would often switch my position at the last minute, knowing the other teams had worked hard to match talent for talent on their runners. Often, the other teams scrambling to adjust would give us a distinct advantage.

The older I got, the harder I worked to be the popular kid, the cool kid, the funny kid, the good-looking kid, the fastest kid, on and on. I would do or say whatever it took to be *that guy* in any room. But what so often happens is that all those worlds start to blend together. Before long, I couldn't keep up the charade I had created. I would forget who I was supposed to be in front of this person or that person. Bottom line—I had become a fake everywhere.

Free Falls and Throw Up

Shooting my mouth off to try to impress people finally caught up with me on the morning of my eighteenth birthday.

For years, I had told everyone that I wanted to go skydiving. I thought it was a huge, extravagant claim to get people to respond exactly the way I wanted by saying, "Gary, you're crazy!" or "That's too dangerous!" or "Dude, you're insane!" But there was just one problem: I had never put any thought into what that experience would actually be like. It was always a "someday" thing. I never had any real intentions of jumping out of a plane, but skydiving sounded cool—and I thought saying I wanted to do it made me look cool.

At 7:00 a.m. sharp on the morning of July 15, 1999, my parents burst through my bedroom door while I was still sound asleep, announcing, "Gary, wake up! It's your birthday! Surprise! . . . We're taking you skydiving!" *Evidently the legal age for tandem skydiving in the state of Florida is eighteen. Who knew? . . . Obviously, my parents!*

Attempting to wake up, realizing what they were saying, I began to think, *Holy crap! No!!! This cannot be happening!*

I'm sure that for many months my parents had been having a blast covertly mapping out their surprise birthday gift for me. I could just hear them: "Gary is going to be so pumped that we are finally helping him fulfill his dream of skydiving! This is going to be so great!"

After years of airing my teenage bucket list to everyone, now I was too far down the road to turn back. The jig was up. I had to go through with it. Still bleary-eyed from the early morning wake-up call, I got in the car with my extremely excited parents and headed to the municipal airport in Titusville, where good money had been laid down to pay for my eighteenth-birthday adventure.

After checking in, we noticed a very small female walk out of the hangar toward the plane.

"Wow, she looks like she's about thirteen or fourteen. Really brave of her to go up today," Dad commented. Then he called out to the girl, "Hey, are you skydiving today?"

She stopped, turned, looked at us, and answered, "No, I'm the pilot."

Obviously, she was much older than Dad thought, and she turned out to be an amazing pilot. But, in that moment, the revelation did not help my fear at all.

A group of really awesome-looking guys walked out of the hangar. They were professional sky surfers who were spending the day practicing for the next X-Games, and I was going to be on their plane. If I hadn't known already that I was hopelessly outclassed, that sealed it.

After some brief orientation and instructions, there I was, strapped to a total stranger as the only tandem jumper in a small plane full of X-Gamers, while my parents and a videographer waited below in perfect safety.

During my ninety-second free fall, I had a short but strong conversation with myself about my people-pleasing habits. I also made all kinds of empty promises to God about what I'd do for Him if He would just get me down to the ground in one piece.

Here's what no one tells you about skydiving. (If you have ever done it and loved it, good for you; please just allow me this moment, okay?) When the parachute suddenly opens as you are plummeting straight toward the ground at 120 miles per hour, it immediately reverses your fall and violently jerks you right back up—which can leave your innards feeling very distressed. Because of this insane feat of physics, skydiving instructors actually teach you how to throw up. (No, I am not kidding.)

My instructor had told me, "Gary, if you feel like you're about to throw up, tap on the skydiver's leg that you're attached to on the tandem. He'll move his head one way and you stick your head out the other way and just let it rip." Sure enough, when the chute opened, my stomach felt betrayed and chose full-on revenge. Thankfully, I remembered my "training" and tapped on the guy's leg. I leaned opposite him and threw up—*straight up*. After you vomit, of course, your eyes water. When you vomit while skydiving, the goggles you're wearing then fill up with tears and you can't see a thing. There's also that unmistakable taste from hell in your mouth. Sounds like fun, huh?

Here was the worst part for me on my first day as an eighteen-year-old whose main goal was to look cool: As I mentioned before, my parents had a videographer recording the whole thing, so the entire experience was caught on tape. When my tandem partner and I very ungracefully hit the ground, I literally collapsed and went into the fetal position, traumatized and nauseated. After we slid to a stop, the video guy came running over to me, camera rolling, and called out, "Gary! What was it like?!"

I looked at him and boldly said, "I will *never* . . . do *that* . . . again!"

You aren't going to see videos like mine posted on skydiving websites because they are not good for business. I think any activity in which they have to teach you how to throw up needs to be seriously considered beforehand!

But my parents loved the entire adventure. They laughed and laughed, certainly getting their money's worth out of my birthday gift. To this day, I think they knew I really didn't want to go skydiving and decided to call my bluff.

MercyMe Plus One

In the middle of my senior year of high school, our church youth group made our annual trip to a Shepherd Ministries Student Conference where, at that time, Dawson McAllister was always the main speaker. At one of the sessions, they announced they were taking applications for summer internships, so I decided to apply to work at one of their camps. A couple of months later, they called to say I was accepted.

My Christian identity was the one that always got me the most approval, so I knew when I graduated from high school that people would be more impressed to find out I was going to work for a full-time ministry than getting a track scholarship to some small local college. Pretending to be a really good Christian while knowing in my heart how badly I fell short was very common for me at the time. That's what religion does when you don't understand that God wants a relationship with us, not a performance from us.

In May 2000, I graduated from high school. Two weeks later, I loaded up my truck and moved to Irving, Texas, outside Dallas where Shepherd Ministries is based. We had two weeks of summer camps, two weeks off, and then two more weeks of camp.

While I was back home in Florida during the two weeks between camps, Shepherd called to ask if I would be interested in taking a full-time job as a conference promoter starting in the fall. Having attended all their events for the past five years, I was very familiar with the culture and accepted the offer, feeling very excited.

When I went back to Dallas for the final two weeks of camp, I took all my belongings with me to make my first official move away from home. Much of the Shepherd staff went to Irving Bible Church, so I started attending there and volunteered in the children's ministry. But I also began to make some friends outside of church and work. These different circles caused the chameleon in me to keep changing colors in my new location. Even while establishing life on my own, I continued juggling different personas.

In addition to my intense need for affirmation, I also had a massive fear of rejection. While those two dynamics definitely work hand-in-hand, they also work against one another. Unfortunately, both would stay with me well into my adult life.

While in Dallas, I lived with two other guys. One was Ryan Slaughter, who ran video for Shepherd; the other was a guitarist named Mike Scheuchzer, who played for a new up-and-coming band that was leading worship at our conferences. They went by the name of MercyMe.

I worked for Shepherd for about a year. Toward the end of that season, the ministry began a transition into a new organization called Planet Wisdom, which meant everyone who worked for Shepherd would be laid off. They offered all employees a chance to be rehired. I didn't want to deal with the changeover, so in the summer of 2001 I decided to continue my education at Troy State University in Alabama.

I was picking up a few things at Walmart a few weeks before starting school when I got a call from a number I didn't recognize. When I answered, the guy said, "Hey, Gary, this is Bart Millard with MercyMe."

I had gotten to know all the guys from the band at the conferences. Bart told me they signed with a manager in Nashville and landed a record deal. Since they now had a little more money, they had decided to hire someone to travel with them to manage selling their merchandise (merch) at shows and asked if I'd be interested. Hitting the road with a band sounded way cooler than going to college, so I accepted on the spot.

At that time, the band still lived in north Texas, so I flew to Dallas to meet up with them. The guys picked me up in their 1973 Silver Eagle tour bus with no AC. We drove straight to a summer camp in Glorieta, New Mexico, where they were leading worship for the week.

My job with the band was fairly straightforward: When we arrived at a venue, they would head to the stage to set up their instruments and do sound check while I got all the merch ready to sell. Then, along with the help of a few volunteers, I sold their product until the end of the night, then packed up all that remained for the next show. I also kept inventory and placed orders.

During that first week, the guys got a call from their new manager, Scott Brickell. He told them that as soon as they were finished at Glorieta, they needed to head to Nashville, where their label was throwing a big release party for the new record, *Almost There*; one of the songs was called "I Can Only Imagine."

After arriving in Nashville, we went to the top floor of a high-rise building near downtown for the party. The management team, record label reps, and people from the Christian music industry were there. Surveying the room of who's-whos and the incredible view out the massive glass windows that overlooked Music City was a surreal experience for me.

All this took place in my first two weeks on the job. I was back home in Dallas on an off day, driving down the road by myself, when their first single, "Bless Me, Indeed," came on the radio for the first time. (We were all listening to the local Christian station all the time, because we knew they were going to play the song at some point.) When it did, we all called each other, freaking out.

When "I Can Only Imagine" was released as their next single, the band was off to the races. The song was a massive hit that went on to become a Christian classic and eventually led to a movie about Bart's life story. Life would never be the same for them.

The crazy explosion of MercyMe's popularity quickly created some good growing pains. Within six months, they were playing much bigger shows that required more technical help—but I have never been a "techie." While the guys and I were having a lot of fun, I could see what they needed was not anything I could provide. They saw it, too, and knew some changes had to be made. We mutually agreed to part ways but committed to staying friends. Because I decided to stay in Dallas to find a new job, I still occasionally went out on the road with them to help when they needed an extra hand.

The merch job may have only lasted a little while, but for the past twenty-plus years, our friendship has not only remained, but become closer and stronger. We had no idea at that time how my relationship with the band would literally change everything for me in such a dramatic way after I had gone through some of the worst days of my life.

A Prophet in His Hometown

Because Mike Scheuchzer and I were still roommates, eventually MercyMe's bus driver and sound man moved in with us, too. While taking a few classes at a community college, I went to work in the children's ministry at Irving Bible Church.

Working on a minister's salary while struggling with approval created a real conflict for me: I wasn't making the money to go with the lifestyle I was trying to live. My pride wouldn't allow me to admit to anyone that I was living far beyond my means.

I was making only the minimum payments on my credit card debt—and sometimes using one card to pay another one. With every month that passed, the problem was compounding. Literally. Within two years, I had amassed $20,000 in debt. It was awful. Worse than skydiving. More than once when a new bill arrived, throwing up was involved.

I will never forget sitting on the floor of my apartment in Dallas, staring at bills with huge numbers I thought I could never possibly repay. Realizing I had to stop the madness, I swallowed my pride and called Dad. Through tears of shame, I confessed the trouble I had gotten myself into, and said, "Dad . . . I need your help."

Thankfully, just like the father in the story of the Prodigal Son, my dad met me with his arms wide open and showed me a lot of grace. He said, "Gary, let's consolidate your debt and I'll help you get back on your feet. But you'll have to move back home to stop the financial bleeding."

While I hadn't blown my inheritance like the young prodigal Jesus talked about in the legendary parable, I understood what it felt like to have to humble myself and go back home with my tail tucked between my legs because of irresponsibility and bad decisions. I got a job at a local oil change shop and began paying off my debt.

Like many other churches, ours—Rockledge Baptist—decided to change its name to something that carried a little less cultural stigma, eventually rebranding itself as Grace Fellowship. Same building, same people, new sign. Dad hadn't been the youth pastor for a while, and the church's current one had just left to go to seminary, so there was an opening.

I applied for the position; the fact that I was following in my father's footsteps with some résumé clout from Shepherd Ministries and Irving Bible College gave me a boost, and the committee decided to hire me. That's how I became the full-time youth pastor at the church where I grew up. Full circle. All four gospels in the New Testament give the account of the first time Jesus went back to his hometown. In Luke 4:24, we find His powerful quote: "But I tell you the truth, no prophet is accepted in his own hometown." (A bit of foreshadowing here.)

My full name is actually Gary Miracle Jr., so everybody in Rockledge called me Junior to differentiate me from my father. That was totally fine with me—until I took the job as the youth pastor. Being Junior to Senior meant that I could never fully get out of Dad's shadow with the church. They never allowed me the respect or authority he had enjoyed. I certainly *wasn't* claiming to be a prophet, but I *was* trying hard to be the youth pastor!

For example, if there were any big decisions to be made that had to do with the youth group, the other pastors would get together, make them without me, and then inform me what I was to do. I was never part of the leadership team. Because my parents were, of course, still going to the church, the most difficult thing was when they would call my dad to get his advice instead of mine. Nothing hostile ever occurred, and Dad and I were always close, but it definitely created an awkward dynamic.

Eventually, seeing that the situation would not change, with my debt paid off and my finances back in order, I decided it was time to leave home again. I was twenty-six years old, in that awkward season when you certainly aren't a kid anymore, but you're also not sure what being an adult looks like yet. I had learned some hard lessons from my many mistakes and gotten back on my feet. Now, even though I would likely fail again at some point, I knew it was time for me to walk out into the world on my own.

CHAPTER TWO

Business, Babies, and the Battle

In 2008 I moved to Louisville, Kentucky, to live with a buddy who was going to seminary. Like most Floridians, I had never really experienced all four seasons. For us, each year is divided in half—hurricane season from June to November, and non-hurricane season from December to May. Michigan was still a long way from Florida, that was for sure.

The first job I landed was at a golf course—something we have plenty of in the Sunshine State. But as fall was starting to give in to the first freezing temps of winter, I was told it would soon be shutting down for a few months to avoid the weather that could quickly turn to snow and ice. I had never thought about how hard it is to tee off into a sixty-mile-an-hour wind driven by an arctic blast, or how easy it is to lose a golf ball in a snow drift. So I started looking for another job.

In December, sitting inside my apartment with the heater on full blast, I found a local sales position at AT&T, submitted my application, and was contacted right away for an interview. To my surprise, I was offered the job on the spot and invited to report in for training the next day at 9:30 a.m. to shadow a guy who was already doing the job. Ready to get to work, I accepted. The next morning, I reported to the office a few minutes early, dressed to kill in my best suit and tie. From what I knew about sales, the first rule is to make a strong impression on your clients before you even say a word.

As soon as I met the guy they wanted me to shadow for the day, he said, "Okay, Gary, let's go." I thought, *Alright, I wonder which nice, warm office is his? Which cozy spot is he taking me to start learning the ropes?* Realizing we were headed for the front door, I asked, "Uh, where we going?" He just answered, "To my car." Right away, I was concerned for my safety and confused about what was happening, but decided to just stay quiet, wait, and see. Remember, I'd only been told to report to an office at 9:30 a.m. for training. Assuming I was going to be inside a building with a heater on all day, I hadn't even brought a coat. No gloves or hat. In fact, since this was my first winter outside Florida, I didn't own anything more than a light jacket. I was wearing an undershirt, a dress shirt, suit coat, and pants with shiny dress shoes.

As we drove out of the parking lot, not only was it snowing, but the local bank's marquee thermometer said it was seven degrees. In Florida, a seven in Fahrenheit always has another number behind it, somewhere between zero and nine. Single-digit temps! This was crazy.

As we drove into a nice suburb, my trainer explained that from 10:00 a.m. to 7:00 p.m. we were going door-to-door trying to talk people into switching their home internet service to AT&T. This was the "sales job." Immediately, I looked to see if he had locked the car doors and began to calculate how bad it might hurt if I jumped out of the car at thirty miles per hour. Maybe I could dive out at the next stop sign? Stop, drop, and roll.

We pulled onto a street of nice homes as far as you could see, parked the car at the curb, and got out into the bitter cold. The wind hit me like a prizefighter's punch, cutting right through my suit to remind me that I was an idiot for not bringing a coat. You know, just in case we ventured out for a nice corporate lunch. And gloves. I would have given a hundred dollars for a decent pair of gloves right then. When the snowflakes hit my face, they actually stung. They might look pretty and harmless, but those suckers can hurt you, like tiny ninja stars being thrown into your cheeks. I began to question my judgment for ever crossing my home state line to leave the land of snowbirds and alligators.

But with arms crossed, hands tucked into my pits, and every part of me freezing, I followed the guy down the sidewalk as he started knocking on doors. My only responsibility was to smile, look friendly, keep my mouth shut, listen, and learn. The obvious added challenge today was that even if someone was at home, they wouldn't want to open their door to let the heat out and the cold in. Yet, here we were, trying to convince people to do just that. I secretly prayed for a lonely little old lady to invite us in for hot chocolate and cookies, and then maybe hold us hostage.

For the next several hours I followed that guy like a new puppy, watching him knock on doors and make his pitch. I was impressed, because he was definitely committed. While I was uncertain about my future, I knew I was 100 percent miserable going door-to-door.

Finally, unable to feel my face, I looked at my trainer, and said, "No offense, man, but I've had enough. There's absolutely no way I'm taking this job. Please give me your keys. I'm going back to the car to wait for you to finish out your day." With a look on his face that landed somewhere between "Hey, man, I get it," and "Really, wimp? You're quitting already?" he blankly nodded and handed over his keys.

On my walk back to the car, I arrived at the obvious conclusion that, the day before, the manager failing to tell me to dress appropriately for the weather was only to assure I would at least show up. After a few very, very long hours sitting in the car, I saw the trainer walking back. I was amazed that he was still mobile and not frozen. Finally, this horrible day was about be over. We made our way in silence down the snowy roads back to the office.

My trainer escorted me into the boss's office and explained what had happened. To my surprise, the manager showed what an amazing salesman he was, because, by the end of the talk, he had dangled enough money and incentives in front of me to convince me to take the job.

Remember when I told you I was a people-pleaser? That personality fault often caused me to put myself in a tough spot to avoid looking bad in the moment, kicking the can of reality down the road for another day.

No Place Like Home

While working at AT&T in 2009, I met the woman who became my first wife.

After a couple of months of dating, we got engaged. Then six months later, we married. Before long, we found out she was expecting, and on January 19, 2011, my first son—Asher—was born. To make more money for our growing family, I left the residential grind and switched to the business sales division. While still a tough gig, at least I was no longer trying to get into people's homes. Most businesses have an open door where you can walk right in and start talking. Then, from there, you just have to get to the decision-maker.

Eventually, I saw how working at an AT&T consumer store selling cell phones would allow me to go to work at the same location every day. I put in for a transfer, and in November 2011 was accepted at a store in Titusville, Florida, about twenty minutes from where I grew up. We now had additional support from my extended family, who surrounded us and ten-month-old Asher with love.

In 2012, we found out we were pregnant with our second son, Ellis. Fortunately, by this point, my job brought in enough money to allow my wife-at-the-time to stay home. We were all so excited.

But on Christmas Day, when she was seven months along, my wife-at-the-time became concerned when she hadn't felt Ellis moving in some time. She went to the doctor first thing the next morning. (December 26 would become a crucial date for me.)

Just as I was about to walk out the door, she called from the emergency room and, through tears, said, "They can't find a heartbeat." I lost it. I was so emotional and distraught that my dad, who had just arrived at our house, had to drive me to the hospital.

The memory of walking into that exam room will be forever burned into my brain. The doctor and his staff were standing around the bed consoling her. I looked over at the sonogram monitor to see a still image of the outline of a child. No movement. No telltale washing machine sounds from the heartbeat on the monitor speaker. Only silence. They explained that the umbilical cord had become wrapped around his neck, cutting off life support. While this is common, particularly with males, only about 10 percent of stillbirths are actually caused by this condition. The doctor sympathetically offered us our options—perform a C-section and remove the baby right away or allow the pregnancy to naturally carry on to completion. After everyone left the room, we talked and decided on the C-section to not prolong the inevitable outcome.

Ellis died in the womb at twenty-eight weeks.

I never got the opportunity to meet him or even see him in person. If you have suffered a miscarriage, a stillbirth, or the death of a child outside the womb, I understand your deep sense of loss. Sympathy is feeling sorry for someone when you haven't experienced the tragedy yourself. Empathy is feeling someone's pain from firsthand knowledge. I know the incredible excitement when you first find out about a child, and I know the horrific hurt you feel when you find your worst fears as a parent have come to pass. Knowing that life is being formed is so real, but then experiencing the death of a child causes the mind to struggle to accept the truth and the heart to battle with the pain. It's devastating. Confusing. Life-altering. And while time does slowly heal us, the what-if questions will likely never stop.

Because of how badly I was hurting, for a while I isolated myself from everyone. I remember screaming. I remember crying. I remember being angry and confused and frustrated about why or how this could happen. If you're a Christ-follower like me, or even just believe there is a God, this is a dilemma. It's so hard to see what He could possibly be doing in the midst of such a tragedy. It's tough to understand why He allows that kind of suffering. I certainly haven't figured this out and have no great spiritual answer to offer. But as we keep working through my story, I will continue to be honest about the tough questions we sometimes have about why bad things happen. I have come to accept that there are just some answers we won't get on this side of Heaven.

Yet here's what I do know: We can trust in the One who does have the answers and holds tomorrow. In John 16:33, Jesus states, "Here on earth you will have many trials and sorrows. But take heart, because I have overcome the world." Look at the promise: "You *will* have trials and sorrows." But then comes Jesus's offer: You can "take heart, because I have overcome the world." For some reason, we tend to take advantage of our relationship with God as if we can only take the good without the bad. We must realize that He's simply helping us navigate through all the highs and lows of life in His mercy and grace.

Ellis's original due date was March 22, 2012. But before that date arrived, my wife-at-the-time and I found out we were pregnant again. Looking at the timeline, I had to come to realize that had Ellis been born, I would not have my second son, Walter, who was born on December 19, 2012. I do feel some guilt, because obviously I would give up my own life for Walter, but I also don't want to take anything away from Ellis's short-lived life either. I'm so sad about Ellis, but then I'm so excited to have Walter. But I can't have both.

There are two special kinds of babies: a "sunshine baby," who is born into a family before you encounter a loss, or a "rainbow baby," one born after a sibling died in stillbirth or miscarriage. My parents had a rainbow baby: Me. They had lost a boy eight and a half months into the pregnancy. I was Mom and Dad's next and final child. Then my wife-at-the-time and I had a rainbow baby,

Walter. I was trying to process all this, asking, "What should I be thankful for? Death as well as life? Just part of it or all of it?" I think the word "torn" is the best description for how that feels. Balancing such tough emotions is one of the hardest things we have to deal with as flawed people. Personally, all I can do is trust that God has a different plan than mine, but then His always works out the best in the end. Isaiah 55:9 reminds us, "My ways are higher than your ways and my thoughts higher than your thoughts."

The day after we lost Ellis, all the guys in MercyMe reached out. Robby, the drummer, called and said, "Hey, I want you to hear a song we've been working on. Unfortunately, all I have for you to listen to right now is Bart's vocals over my drums. There's no music cut yet."

While in one way, because the song was not finished, it was the worst-sounding song I've ever heard in my life, in another, it was one of the most beautiful. The lyrics met my emotions and touched my heart in a powerful way.

The song was "The Hurt and the Healer." To this day, when I hear that song on the radio or at one of their live shows, the tough memory of those difficult days comes rushing back. But then I am also quickly reminded of the beautiful village I have around me that stepped in to speak hope and encouragement in the midst of my pain.

I once heard someone refer to the season when a young married couple is focused on developing careers and having a family as "business and babies." I want to add a very real aspect to that phrase: the battle. The constant thread through that season is working hard to pay the bills and trying to get ahead, all while fighting the daily battle against the things that barge in unannounced and pull the rug out from under us.

Relationships, Not Transactions

In the middle of all that, I transferred from the store in Titusville to one in Melbourne, Florida. Then AT&T offered me the store manager position in Merritt Island. My climb up the company ladder was finally reaching a top rung: I took over what is known as a "Level Three Corporate Store." With my wife-at-the-time and two boys at home, I felt like I had finally realized the American Dream. I was on top of the world.

The next year, we found out we were pregnant with our third boy, Henry; he was born on June 9, 2014. I began to have visions of forming my own basketball team, even starting to pick out universities with a plan for scholarships. My next goal was figuring out how they could be drafted into the NBA.

Everything was finally going so right! What could possibly go wrong?

Employment. That's what. In July 2014, when Henry was one month old, my corporate boss called me to her office. When I sat down, she wasted no time and didn't sugarcoat the news that I was being let go, effective immediately. One of the veteran employees was unhappy about some of the changes I had made—and this was the outcome. My boss was very gracious and understanding, but she had no choice.

Up to that point, I had not considered another career. I went home with no idea what I was going to do. I felt helpless. I felt betrayed. I was lost. I was scared. Suddenly, I struggled to even feel like a man. I questioned how I could possibly provide for our family at the level to which we had become accustomed. Like sharing the trauma of losing a child, if you have ever suddenly been derailed in your ability to make a living, I understand the intensity of those feelings too. It's amazing how quickly we can become hopeless in the face of certain circumstances—especially when you know other people are relying on you to come through. But I always have to say that my God is never surprised and can work in, around, and through anything.

I wasted no time in calling everyone I knew, letting them know I was looking for work. I spoke to a good friend who worked at a car dealership in Merritt Island who said, "Gary, I don't know what you want to end up doing, but in the meantime, let's get you over here selling cars. At least you'll have some money coming in, because as soon as you sell a car, you can get paid." My answer was, "Well, that's exactly what I need, so I'm in!"

So I started selling cars. Well, to be more accurate, I *tried* to sell cars. I want to be clear that I have a ton of respect for car salespeople—but I couldn't get past being the annoying guy who chased folks down, trying to talk to them while they kept insisting, "Hey, we're just looking." I felt like a buzzard waiting for roadkill as I sat on a bench under a tree at the entrance to the lot, eyeing every car that pulled in. I understood why so many of them avoided making eye contact with me.

After two weeks and way more than eighty hours, I had sold one car. *One*. Meanwhile, the feelings of not being able to take care of my family were getting worse.

Finally, I went up to the boss's office and confessed, "Hey, I *can't* do this anymore. I don't *want* to do this anymore. This is not working for me. Or you, for that matter, since I've only sold one car. I'm absolutely miserable, so I need to leave and find a different job. But thanks for the opportunity."

Just like my AT&T boss, this manager also decided not to make it easy for me to speak my piece and just walk out. After I finished what I thought was goodbye, he asked, "Okay, Gary, why don't you try the internet department?" At the time, that was still a fairly new aspect of the car business, so I asked him to explain. He answered, "When people are shopping online for cars and they request information on one of our vehicles, that submits a lead that goes to our internet department. The folks there respond, answer questions about the car, then hopefully go on to negotiate a deal or set up an appointment for a test drive. By the time the person comes in, they're usually serious about the car. Sometimes the deal is closed before they even get here."

That sounded better than sitting under a tree, waiting to chase "lookers" down, so I said yes. I figured it was worth a try and told him I would give it a week. I literally left his office and went straight to a desk in front of a computer and a phone. Right away, that felt more like when someone walked into the AT&T store. Usually those customers were ready for a new phone or upgrade—there was no hard sell involved.

Within two weeks, I had sold thirteen cars. Along with the one lot sale, I was able to hit my monthly sales goal. I was back on top of the world with good money coming in again. My wife-at the-time and I didn't miss a beat on paying our bills. I felt like God had come through for me and provided in every possible way.

On the business side, the model of hitting volume goals with other people on our team also fit me really well. It felt a lot like being on the track team: I had to run my race as fast as possible to get my medal, but the team also had to do well for all of us to win. I recall one particular month, we were down to the wire on the last day, and if we sold two more cars, the dealership would get a bonus of $180,000. At that point, you can make someone an incredible deal because the goal is so much bigger than losing money on one sale.

Over time, I also was able to build relationships with a lot of customers—some of whom are still in my life. After a while, I began to realize that being a successful salesperson is really about being honest and doing the right thing for the client, not just making a transaction. Some salespeople put customers into cars they can't really afford, just to make the bigger commission. Like getting someone into a $600 payment when $400 would be best. I realized I had to work toward the long run, not just the here and now. Thinking marathon, not sprint.

MercyMe even got involved in my car sales. Well, to be fair, I involved them. Anytime I found out that a customer was into Christian music, I would ask if he or she had heard of the band. If they had—especially with a comment like, "Oh my gosh, I'm a huge fan!"—then it was game on. I would send a text to the guys that said something like, "Hey, I'm trying to sell a car to a fan. Can you send me a message or a selfie for them? Help me out here." Every single time, at least one (and sometimes all) of them would respond—especially if they were on the road, on the bus, or at a venue together.

A few times, they sent audio messages for me to play for the customer—and, of course, they were always comedians about it. Once, Bart sent back a picture of him holding up a sign that read, "I don't know who Gary Miracle is. Please tell him to stop calling me!" I was always grateful for their help, because they also made it more fun for my customers. Those guys have always been there for me, no matter what life has thrown my way.

Landing the Dream Job

By October of 2017, after three years in the internet department, one day I was taking a break, hanging out and visiting with some of the salespeople on the lot, when a man pulled up, got out of his car, and asked to speak to the owner or the general manager. I escorted him in and dropped him off at the secretary's desk. A few minutes later, I overheard him say he was the district manager with Autotrader, the massive internet car dealer. "We just lost our sales rep for this territory," he was saying. "If you know of anybody, please send them my way."

I was intrigued.

I hung out around the corner, waiting for the guy to walk back to his car. As soon as he did, I said, "Hey, I don't know if I was supposed to hear what you said, but I'm interested in that position." He smiled and answered, "Well, it would be a conflict of interest if I recruited you from a car dealership, but here's my business card. Give me a call sometime and we can chat."

I didn't waste any time; I called him later that afternoon. He repeated, "Again, I can't recruit you, but I can't stop you from going to Autotrader.com to apply for the position."

I went online and did as he suggested. Three weeks later, I had a phone interview that went very well. Then I had a face-to-face interview with the guy I had met at my dealership. In November, I took a day off to meet with him in Orlando. The Monday after Thanksgiving, he called to offer me the position. After I accepted, he said that he would have to get back to me with a start date.

There were three reasons I was really excited about this opportunity: The base pay was more than I made at the car dealership and the benefits were incredible; I could telecommute from home; and it was a nine-to-five, five days a week job. That meant my seventy-hour work weeks would be a thing of the past! No more slaving away on weekends and holidays while my family was at home without me.

The first week of December, my new boss called and said, "Okay, Gary, I have good news and bad news. The good news is you still have the job. Bad news is they put us on a hiring freeze through the holidays and I can't promise you when it will be lifted." That freaked me out a bit, but I didn't want to lose the opportunity. I told him I would wait it out.

A couple of days before Christmas, he called to report that the freeze had been lifted and I could start on January 3, 2018. I was simultaneously relieved and absolutely pumped. The next morning, I went into the dealership to put in my two-week notice. This time, something happened that I didn't see coming. My boss got really angry and yelled, "Pack up your stuff and get out of here! You're fired!"

After I got over my shock, it hit me: For the first time ever, I would have the holidays off to spend with my family. My new job was waiting for me in January, so all was well. This was a huge blessing in disguise. No, I wouldn't make any money over the next two weeks, but I would actually be able to enjoy Christmastime and celebrate New Year's with my kids.

My job with Autotrader was incredible. I was able to work from home. I was able to provide well for my family. To this day, I wouldn't want to work for any other company. Cox Enterprises, the entity that owns Autotrader, is simply an amazing place to work.

Another blessing was that I was the only rep in Florida who lived in the territory he represented. My farthest client was only a forty-minute drive away. On any given day, I could visit as many as ten dealerships. (My goal was to visit each client at least twice a month.) I had forty-five stores on my watch, but I could see all of them every week if I wanted—and because I had lived in the area for so long, I already knew a lot of those people. Some of them were friends from school!

I finally had my dream job, with no thought whatsoever that anything might prevent me from doing what I loved. Of course, something later would. But before we get to that, let me tell you about a life-changing trip I took to Colombia, South America.

CHAPTER THREE

We're Best Friends Forever

In my new job with Autotrader, I felt like my life had been given back to me. With my weekends open for the first time in years, I was able to get involved with my boys' sports teams on Saturdays, become a regular at church again on Sundays, and plug into the life of a community of believers at a level I was never able to before. And with my newfound peace and regular schedule, I started feeling an urgency to address my issue with people-pleasing. My chameleon-like behavior had always plagued me as I wrestled with my own sense of identity. I knew there was never going to be a better time to work on me than now. Some things in my life had to be made right, especially before I faced any other crisis or tragedy.

I began to look inward and ask some hard questions, like, *I know who I've been, and I know who I want to be, but who am I now?* I knew I needed to move beyond just being my family's provider; I had to work on becoming the spiritual leader they needed and deserved. An honest realization I had was, *While I haven't done anything terrible, I also haven't set an intentional example for my kids*. I was definitely ready to go to a deeper level in my relationship with Christ.

One of my first discoveries about my spiritual life was that I had taken on the faith of my parents more than I had established my own, which is very common for kids raised in the church. That is also why so many young people who move away or go off to college so quickly abandon their faith—because it was never their own to start with. My family's faith had always encouraged and spurred me on. I wanted what they had. But there is a major difference between following someone else's Christian example and actually following Jesus. Like the seed Christ spoke of in Matthew 13 that was scattered in shallow soil or among the thorns, my faith never had roots of its own. I realized that I had just been going through the motions, saying and doing things I thought I was supposed to say and do as a Christian, which proved to be superficial. But I wasn't just fooling other people; I was also fooling myself.

As a teenager at church on Wednesday nights in the youth group, I had been the drummer in the worship band, my hands held high in between drum fills. I also was the kid going to the parties on Friday nights after the football game who would hold a beer (but never take a drink because I thought it was disgusting). Wherever I was, I wanted to look cool. I wanted to fit in. But regardless of what I did on weekend nights, I would be right back at church on Sunday morning, playing that part. I became really good at blending into any environment. While I never got into any actual trouble, I always got away with too much and never had any true accountability. I was a natural salesman—really good at talking my way into or out of almost anything with almost anyone.

It was time for all that to end.

The Cure

My new journey of addressing my identity led to two crucial decisions: First, I had to engage my spiritual life by getting involved in my church beyond just a Sunday morning experience. Second, I needed some personal one-on-one discipleship to work through some of my identity issues. The answer to the first issue was obvious: dive into church and the life of the Body of Christ throughout the week. For the second, once again, I turned to my dear friend Bart Millard, who had become a spiritual mentor and had recently dealt with a lot of his past. I knew he was experiencing a new place of maturity in receiving and accepting God's grace.

For a very long time, I had felt like something wasn't right in my faith. Something wasn't connecting in my Christian life. But what was missing? One thing I knew for sure was that I had far too many things hidden in my heart—things I'd done that nobody knew about, things that were eating away at me, causing guilt and shame. Bart had been raised in a denomination where, especially back in the day, there was much more emphasis on behavior: doing the right things and avoiding the wrong things, checking boxes more than actually changing one's heart. Now, he was actively trying to let go of religion and lean into his relationship with Jesus in a way he never had before. I was drawn to and intrigued by his new walk of faith, so we began an ongoing conversation about God's grace and the freedom Jesus died to give us.

Bart took me through a book called *The Cure* by John Lynch. The author asked a question that radically changed my perspective: "What if even on your worst day, when you feel like everything's hitting the fan, Christ is still crazy about you?"

At the time, I couldn't imagine even considering that thought, much less believing it. But the concept absolutely leveled me. I thought, *So, you mean while I'm beating myself up about mistakes, Jesus is still crazy about me?! How could that possibly be true?! You mean I don't have to do all of the "right things" to earn His love? I don't have to not sin as much? I don't have to reach a quota of behavior to get His approval? You mean to say He loves me regardless of my behavior?* That possibility blew my mind. I kept reading Lynch's words, thinking they might somehow change to what I had always believed to be true about God. But they didn't.

Another game-changing question was, "What if you found out that, even when you confess your sin and your struggles, God still loves you and won't judge you?" I finally had to close the book and go for a walk around the block to let this new truth sink into my heart. *What if I decide to actually believe these statements about God's love for me? What if I start to live like they are true? What would change about my life?*

Even though I had asked Jesus into my heart as a kid, had been a youth pastor on a church staff, and traveled with a Christian band, I came to the honest conclusion that I had always spiritually coasted. But now, finally, everything was beginning to make sense *to me* about what Jesus had done *for me*. It was a slow process, but I was letting go of everyone else's expectations and accepting that I only needed to be the man Jesus died and rose again for me to become. I didn't need all my many contrived images or anyone else's ideal; I just had to be transformed into Christ's image.

I don't want to discredit my moment of salvation back in 1991 as a kid in church. I know Jesus saved me then. But now, as an adult, I was truly surrendering to His Lordship. The "something" I knew I was missing had finally arrived.

Scriptures like Jeremiah 29:13 began to have new meaning: "You will seek me and find me when you seek me with all your heart" (NIV). I decided it was high time to give promises like that a try and believe they were written for me. I chose to seek Christ with all my heart and not look to anyone else for my identity. Not my parents. Not my pastor. Not my friends. Not even Bart. No more trying to impress people by my life, but simply expressing Christ through my life.

The places I once went, the words I once used, the jokes I once made, and the things I once watched no longer held any appeal for me because of my pursuit of Him. As a result, the shame and guilt that had been weighing me down began to slowly diminish.

A radical change in my Christian worldview was taking place. I will always be grateful to Bart for expending so much energy and time pouring into my life in a way very few ever have. He is one of the greatest communicators of the truth of the Gospel I've ever heard.

I can vividly recall thinking in that season, *God, what are You going to do with my life? How can You possibly use me and my testimony?*

Living by Faith, Not by Sight

My spiritual growth led to a deeper involvement in church and ministry. I started facilitating a community group at our house every Friday night—sometimes with as many as eleven families and about thirty kids, all age ten and under.

Our church was involved in a two-year-long Calvary Chapel program called the School of Ministry. By September 2016, I decided that some formal training would be the right move to equip me to reach more people, so I applied and was accepted.

One of our early assignments was to listen to all of Pastor Chuck Smith's verse-by-verse teaching through the Bible, from Genesis to Revelation. So I started listening to those every morning at 5:00 a.m. I also tuned in exclusively to Christian music while driving around for work. I surrounded myself with Jesus, getting to know Him as a Person in a relationship that I had up until that point not understood was possible.

During my second year in the school, I experienced the only vision from the Lord I've had so far in my life. There was no denying that what I "saw" wasn't just my own thoughts or imagination. I'll tell you the details in a moment, but here's the spiritual-to-practical connection: One of the graduation requirements for my program was to go on a mission trip outside the U.S. I had never traveled for any reason other than work or vacation, so the idea of such an adventure was intimidating. Even though our church was constantly sending teams to other countries, I had a hard time deciding where to go. But I 100 percent knew the vision was connected to the mission trip. Here's why.

When I was a youth pastor, I had a great relationship with my senior pastor. He and his wife were caring for the newborn baby of someone in their extended family so the child wouldn't be placed into foster care. I was sitting with them and their two sons—both of whom were in college—in his office one evening, talking about their decision to move forward with adoption. I remember being amazed at their unified commitment as a family. Curious, I asked, "So, why did you do it? At a time in your life when you're older and your guys here are grown, why would you decide to take in a baby?" Their youngest son immediately answered, "Because we're Christians. It's what we're supposed to do."

His words were a cross between a spiritual revelation and an emotional gut-punch.

In that moment, I realized that whomever I ended up marrying and whatever my family might look like, adoption and foster care had to be in my future, too. Immediately, this crazy peace came over me and I promised myself and God, *I'm going to adopt one day*. It wasn't a legalistic thing. Not a have-to, but a get-to. James 1:27 commands us to step up for the widows and orphans in some way, and I knew I wanted to be part of a permanent solution for a child.

Now, to explain my vision: One night in February 2018, I was lying in bed, my thoughts bouncing between my foreign mission trip and adoption. All these years later, the calling was still there. I had never pursued the topic with my family, because I wanted us to have all our own kids first before adopting. I wanted that child to be the youngest.

Desperately wanting God's direction, I remembered Jeremiah 29:13, "You will seek me and find me when you seek me with all your heart." I decided to read my Bible and as I opened it, the vision immediately began. It was very short, but very specific. Even though my eyes were wide open, I "saw" dirt roads running through some trees in the mountains, with Jeeps driving back and forth on them. That was it: several Jeeps driving on tree-lined dirt roads in a mountainous area. (I know it doesn't sound very spiritual. There were no angels. Nothing heavenly at all.)

Within seconds, I snapped out of it and wondered what in the world had happened. *What does this mean, God?* But I knew the mini-movie playing in my mind was somehow connected to my mission trip and meant something for my family.

I went straight to my computer and started searching for places with mountains, trees, and Jeep trails. Of course, everything from Colorado to Zimbabwe came up.

This happened on a Monday night. The next evening, I was sitting in my School of Ministry class. We were halfway through the lesson when the pastor suddenly stopped and looked straight at me, asking, "Gary, have you been on a foreign mission trip yet?"

I answered, "No, I haven't," but I was thinking, *Why are you calling me out in front of everybody?!*

He said, "I'm leading a team to Colombia in August, and I want you to go with me." Still a bit in shock, I just said, "Uh, okay. Great." With that, he picked right back up with his teaching.

But I was shaken. *God, why did that just happen? Colombia? What does this mean?* I don't think I heard another word my pastor said. I instantly began searching Google Earth for a place in Colombia that might match what I had seen in my vision the night before. I was working hard to connect the dots and find an answer.

After class, I quizzed the pastor about the trip. He told me what he knew about the city, the church, and the villages we would visit. When I got home, I started searching again in that specific area.

Nothing came up. Nothing. So I decided not to drive myself crazy; I had to put the whole thing on the back burner and refused to think about it anymore. Oddly enough, all my questions about both the trip and the adoption just stopped. For the next five months, I poured everything I had into the lives of my three boys, with a major focus on coaching their soccer teams. I loved that season with them; it developed into even more time together as their summer vacation began.

First World Meets Third World

My team of a dozen people met at the church at 5:00 a.m. one August morning to depart for Colombia. We loaded our luggage in the shuttle vans and headed to the airport.

I had never gone through customs before, so everything from this point on was a new experience for me. As soon as we got to Colombia and headed into the city of Jamundi, I started scanning the terrain for anything that looked like what I had seen in my vision. Again, nothing matched. I decided I had to let it go and not allow myself to be distracted from my purpose on the trip. I was all in, constantly praying, "God, You have me here. Whatever You want to do with me, let's do it."

On the second day, we visited a small pediatric hospital for children twelve years and younger. All were terminally ill. We talked and prayed with each child through our translator. Like kids in any country, despite their illnesses, they were all smiles. Next, we went to a city park, set up some games, and talked to anyone who would interact with us. Of course, our end goal was to share Jesus with them.

On the third day, we were taken to what locals called "the poor village." Having already seen a great deal of Third World poverty, we wondered how much worse this could be. Our van began the trek that was supposed to be only a few miles outside the city. About halfway there, a police car came up behind us, both lights and siren on. The lead missionary quickly explained that most of the police were corrupt and we should not say a word, make any sudden movements, or give them any sort of resistance. Evidently, two vans loaded with obvious foreigners looked like a great search-and-confiscate opportunity.

We sat there while the cops literally went through all our stuff. Anything they wanted, they took, knowing we couldn't do anything about it. They grabbed personal belongings, as well as supplies we had brought for the village. Once they had pillaged everything they wanted and loaded up their loot, they waved us on. Feeling violated and shaken, we drove on until we got to what looked like a huge farm with a fence and large entry gates. As we pulled up, someone opened them to allow us to drive through.

Here's where it starts to get really interesting—at least for me. As we drove down the farm road, we could see hills covered with large trees in the distance; until eventually, we found ourselves on a dirt road inside a forest. Then, seemingly out of nowhere, we saw several Jeeps drive up behind us and start to pass. It was exactly what I had seen in my vision! Every single detail was there, as if I had been given some kind of prophetic snapshot of this moment in time.

Tears began to stream down my face as I sat looking out the van window. How do you explain this outside of God? At the time, I didn't think I could share what I was experiencing with anyone in the van. I didn't want to sound crazy by saying, "Hey! I've seen this before!" Yet I knew what God had shown me, and I believed Him. He gave me an experience that I can never fully explain and will certainly never forget.

Soon, everyone noticed that I was silent and in tears. The "Gary, what's wrong?" questions began. Rather than mention the vision, I told the truth about my heart for adoption and how I felt like this specific trip was somehow connected to it. A local pastor and his wife who were with us zeroed in and asked if I would tell them more.

So I told them the story about my pastor's family back home and their adoption. I went into detail about how I had wanted to have my own kids first and then adopt a younger child. While I was talking, the pastor's wife looked increasingly surprised. When I finished, she told me that only a week earlier, a beautiful three-year-old girl had come up for adoption in the village we were headed toward. At the time, my youngest son was also three years old. Everyone in the van was blown away by what I was sharing with them. I realized how God was lining up everything exactly with what I had felt compelled to do all those years before—and the vision He had given me was coming to life in real time.

The village looked just like a scene from a TV show or movie; the houses covering the sides of the mountain were mud huts with roofs made of palm fronds. There was no electricity, running water, or bathrooms. If you have been to any Third World country, you've likely seen something similar, but the first time for any Westerner is always an eye-opener.

One very out-of-place sight was what appeared to be an abandoned warehouse. This was where the village children met every morning for the missionaries to teach them.

Of course, after hearing about the little girl, I had tunnel vision in looking for her. But before long, someone found out she was no longer in the village. Crushed and confused, I couldn't understand how God would arrange all those details only for everything to fall apart when we were so close to our goal. I did my best to shake it off and focus on what we were there to do. Toward the end of the day, we loaded up and went back to our base. I felt empty-handed and brokenhearted.

The next day was Friday. That evening, we held one event for men at a private home and another for women at the church. After the guys' event ended, we went back to the church, where I saw all the women were gathered in a tight circle in the middle of the room. When they saw me, they opened the circle to reveal my wife-at-the-time sitting in the center.

She looked at me and said simply, "I just met our daughter."

I was speechless, inwardly freaking out, as the other women began to tell me about this beautiful girl. She had come to the women's ministry meeting, and they had all met her. They said there was a chance she would be at church Sunday morning—and if so, I could meet her then.

I couldn't understand why someone had brought a toddler that was up for adoption to this women's meeting, but I didn't ask any questions. I was just trying to soak in how convinced all those women were that this girl was "the one" for our family.

All day Saturday, my mind raced. I remember praying, "Okay, God, what are You doing? What if this little girl *doesn't* show up at church tomorrow morning? What if no one brings her? What effect will that have on all these women who are so sure about everything they felt regarding this little girl and our adoption? How do we reconcile that? What if she does show up and I meet her, but I don't get the same feeling? What happens then? What if I meet her and love her? What do we do next?" As you can tell, I didn't shut up long enough to give God a lot of room to answer.

That night, when our team met to go over the assignments for church the next day, I was charged with leading the children's ministry. Sunday morning, I was upstairs getting everything ready for the kids to show up when someone came running up the stairs, freaking out, and shouting, "She's here! Gary, she's here! Come down and meet her!"

I felt like I was going to pass out. My knees started shaking.

I went downstairs, turned a corner, and saw her standing there.

I Choose You

I need to let you know that I do not speak any Spanish. I didn't then and I don't now. But I realized immediately that the girl in front of me was not three years old; she was *thirteen* years old, and her name was Johana. (Is there a three in thirteen? Well, yes. Easy to see how that got lost in translation.)

I smiled and eased toward her; I had been told that, because of everything she had gone through in her life, she had a deeply rooted fear of men. I later learned that she had been attending that church for over a year and still wouldn't talk to the pastor. At that point, I was six-foot-two and 240 pounds with a massive beard—probably pretty scary for any kid who didn't know me.

But God was obviously at work because as soon as we locked eyes, Johana walked right to me, buried her head in my chest, and wrapped her arms tightly around my waist, the way a drowning person holds onto a life preserver in the middle of a stormy sea. (I think she still holds the record for the biggest hug I have ever been given.) I looked over at the translator, who by now had tears in his eyes, and said, "Tell her that I want to be her dad."

I knew in that moment, whether she was three or thirteen, I had met my daughter.

I was later told Johana had changed clothes several times that morning, as females will often do when getting ready for something important. She wanted to be sure to wear the perfect outfit that day. She finally chose a shirt that said, "We're Best Friends Forever." That message couldn't have been more perfect for our first meeting.

As people began to show up for church, I had to leave to go lead the children's ministry. But as soon as the service was over, I found the pastor and his wife, who called in Johana's foster mom. With the translator's help, we asked for permission to pursue adoption. She agreed.

When I think back on the season when I changed jobs and felt compelled to deepen my spiritual walk with Christ, I had no idea it was all directly connected to the Lord getting me ready for everything that was coming into my life—my renewed commitment to faith, family, and church; my discipleship with Bart; my training in the School of Ministry; the mission trip; and being at the right place at the right time to meet my daughter.

And in so many ways, Johana is my miracle.

And now, she always will be a Miracle.

CHAPTER FOUR

Five + One = Complete

When I was growing up—and even later, when I was becoming a father—I always had a standing joke: If I ever had a daughter, I wanted to name her either Anita or Juwanna. I loved that combined with my last name, those choices would sound either like a statement ("I need a miracle") or a question ("You want a miracle?"). As with my skydiving story, I told everyone who would listen and always ended with, "How cool would that be?!"

And now, here I was on the way to gaining a daughter with a name pronounced Jah-WA-na. It was, indeed, very cool.

After the mission trip, we were able to tell the boys all about her and how she would be joining our family as soon as we could work out all the details. We were all excited about what God was doing in bringing us a daughter and big sister.

We quickly discovered two huge challenges in the process: time and money. Especially with international adoptions, the journey can be long and incredibly expensive. The Colombian authorities informed us that it could take up to eighteen months and cost as much as $30,000 to bring Johana home. As discouraging as that sounded at the time, it ended up being a conservative estimate. When all was said and done, the ordeal took two and a half years and cost around $65,000—but we knew that when our family was finally complete, the result would be both timeless and priceless.

Through this painful and challenging time, those in our community and network gathered around to support us—an incredible blessing. Oftentimes, people will be gung-ho and help you in the beginning of a process, but then they start to lose interest when the results don't appear quickly. Not so with my tribe. Most of them stood with us to the finish line, and about 80 percent of the costs were covered by gifts given to us out of love. The old saying, "it takes a village," was certainly proven true in our case. But, in the end, everyone involved was blessed to witness God's power at work and experience the unity of the Body of Christ.

Whatever It Takes

We had to go through four different adoption agencies along the way because no one wanted to run the Colombian government's gauntlet; officials don't like international adoptions, so they make the process as difficult as possible. We were always at their mercy, with zero control while attempting to comply with the next demand. This effectively weeds out all but the most committed adoptive parents; along the way, you need to keep being motivated by your love for the child because the path so often looks bleak.

We had to work through every channel we could find and build relationships with "the right people." When we finally neared the end of the process, we were told the entire family—including all our children—had to move to Colombia for thirty days to complete the requirements. Colombia has a lot of regulations in place to protect the child being adopted.

I secured a leave of absence from work, and just before Thanksgiving, all five of us left Florida to spend the required thirty days in Colombia. Three days later, we received a call saying Johana's case worker was ready to place her in our full-time care.

After we arrived and got settled into our apartment in Cali, we waited for what the adoption services call "Gotcha Day," the first time your child is left with your family. They had given us a date and said she would be brought by "in the afternoon." But that morning, there was a knock at the door. I was finishing up getting ready in the bathroom when I heard my kids talking to someone. I walked out to see Johana standing there. Being caught a bit off-guard, the first few minutes were awkward for us and her. But soon, we all began to hug.

The representatives from the adoption agency stayed with us for a few hours, checking us out, going through paperwork, and giving us instructions for our stay. When they left, we were together for the first time as a family. After we ate lunch, all the kids got up on the bed together and watched a *Superman* movie on TV.

The language barrier was very real as we spoke no Spanish and Johana didn't speak English. At first, there were lots of hand motions and pointing with big smiles. Early in the second week, we had to move to a city in the mountains called La Mesa, where there was a court with the judge assigned to our case. Everything continued to go smoothly, and on December 10, 2018, the judge signed Johana's papers, making her officially and legally my daughter—Johana Miracle.

November and December are spring and summer months in the Southern Hemisphere, so it was hot the whole time we were there. And because most of the places we went had no air conditioning, we spent a lot of time outdoors with the locals. My three boys got to meet other kids, play in the parks, and go to local shops and the market. We had no idea that the month we were there would create a family adventure. The language barrier just made it that much more of an educational experience for us all.

During the last two weeks of our stay, we had to go to Bogotá, the capital, to finalize the adoption process and apply for Johana's citizenship papers at the American consulate. This was also called "bonding time." Every other day, people from the adoption agency would come in and talk with Johana, or we would have an appointment at their facility. In the meetings, they would ask questions like, "Do you like your family?" and "Are they treating you well?" If something was not right, especially with her being a nearly fifteen-year-old girl, they wanted to give her every opportunity to speak up.

All the sessions went well as the details were finalized. On December 20, 2018, the Colombian government gave us its full approval; we were free to pack up and go home with our daughter.

Just three days before Christmas, we walked into the baggage claim area back in Florida for the first time as a family of six to find that everyone who had supported our adoption journey was there to meet us. There were balloons and signs and hugs and smiles all around. Everyone had on matching T-shirts that read, "Families don't have to match." (Get it? Matching T-shirts that say . . . never mind.) What a Christmas gift that was!

The first week of January, we enrolled Johana in public school. By that point, she had picked up some English, but by no means was she fluent enough to understand a teacher in any American subject. This may sound cruel, but it was exactly what the adoption agency had told us to do. And it worked, because within a few months, Johana had become fluent in English and was thriving in her new home.

There's one final miraculous detail regarding my kids that I want to share. After we lost Ellis through miscarriage, we buried his ashes on February 3. It turns out that February 3 is also Johana's birthday. So now on that special day, I get to celebrate both of them. What a beautiful, divine combination! It's incredibly special that God would offer me such a granular detail to cling to.

Good Idea, Bad Timing

The next story is really tough for me to share. I could leave it out, but I believe being honest about failures is just as important for inspiration as sharing victories. And because we're all sinners, it's also only fair.

With our biological family complete and Johana's adoption final, I trained to become an officially certified foster parent in the state of Florida. I thought it would be an epic-dad win, but it wasn't at all.

Two days after I was approved, a caseworker called about a seven-year-old girl who had just been removed from her home. She asked if I would take her and, of course, I said yes. Just one month after coming home with Johana, I now had a foster daughter.

Looking back, that was such a horrible decision. We needed to continue to do a lot of work to enfold Johana into our family. But

I just hit the ground running with what I wrongly assumed God was calling me to do. Within a short time, Johana began struggling. I just thought it was because she was still adjusting to our family, school, language, and the culture, but we eventually found out it was because Johana assumed that we were auditioning this other little girl for her place in the family. She thought that, like a used car we were taking for a test drive, we might trade her in for a newer domestic model. With everything that she had been through in her life, her self-image hanging by a thread, she couldn't know any better, especially since her understanding of English was still very limited.

I was heartbroken to realize she thought we were telling her that on one hand, she was our forever daughter, but on the other, she might be sent back to Colombia any day. The pressure she felt was unbearable. Obviously, this news made for a very dark day for me. The last thing I wanted was to hurt any child.

I immediately contacted the foster care agency to explain what we had discovered. I know how harsh this sounds, but we had to put in a request for the little girl to be re-homed, which was horribly unfair to her. The hard lesson God taught me through that very hurtful situation was that a good thing isn't necessarily a God thing. That's why a relationship with Him is so crucial. That's why prayer and waiting to hear clear answers is so critical to making the best decisions. I had been obedient to what He told me to do with Johana, but I strayed from His will on the foster care. As odd as it may sound, becoming a foster parent was not His will because it was not right for Johana, who was clearly my priority at the time.

Once we got our household back in order and Johana understood the truth of our unconditional love for her, she quickly began to thrive. Her English improved by the week. We also saw her and the boys connect in amazing ways—fighting sometimes as brothers and sisters will do—as they bonded. Life became normal overnight. Johana got comfortable enough to complain when she had to go watch them play football, and they would complain when they had to go to her high school soccer games. We became a typical family, griping and protesting, sharing and celebrating.

Life on the Spectrum

There is one other dynamic in our family that I feel is really important for me to share—another unannounced and unforeseen challenge that barged into our lives.

Early in Walter's developmental years, we began to have some concerns about his speech and motor skills. After comparing him to Asher, our firstborn, we decided to talk with our pediatrician. Following that discussion, we all agreed she would order some tests. The results showed that Walter was on the autism spectrum.

While Walter's test results made sense to me, I still struggled for a time to accept them. I soon realized I had to humble myself, needing to do whatever was best for him. I think a huge part of that battle for any parent is just giving your mind and heart the time to accept that this is a condition you will have to learn to navigate like any other challenging diagnosis a loved one may receive. And, of course, there is a huge learning curve in discovering what your child needs moving forward.

We did the necessary research and got Walter into every sort of program we could find. We also applied for every scholarship available to alleviate financial stress. We got him into an Applied Behavior Analysis therapy class at a nearby facility, as well as a speech class at his school. By the time he turned five, he was potty trained, speaking, and doing well in his motor skills. Today, he is thriving. I am grateful for all the people in my life who encouraged me to quit denying reality and accept the "label" of autism so we could get Walter the resources he needed.

I don't know where Walter would be right now emotionally, mentally, or even spiritually had I held onto my pride as a dad. Watching him grow and excel has been a blessing. Learning how his brain works and accepting how God wired him has also been a blessing.

One of my biggest fears arose after I found out how literal someone with autism can be. Being logical is a crucial part of their lives. I became very concerned that the concept of faith in Jesus would be too much for Walter to wrap his brain around. After all, you can't physically see or touch Jesus. There's zero logic in believing in someone you can't see. A lot of people who are *not* on the spectrum can't get beyond that aspect of faith, so for someone with an actual disorder, that can be extremely challenging.

One of the many wonderful things about Florida is a program called the Family Empowerment Scholarship, which allows qualifying children to attend a private school: If one child in your household qualifies, then *all* your children can take advantage of the resources—and ours did.

I am so grateful today to say that all three of my boys have accepted Christ and love Jesus. The Lord is a normal part of our family life. We regularly talk about faith through all the obstacles and hurdles that life can throw at us. Watching Walter come to understand and choose to accept Christ has increased my own faith.

I want to encourage any mom or dad whose child has received a challenging diagnosis that comes with a medical or cultural label: Neither you nor your child are "less than." You didn't do anything wrong. This has nothing to do with you being a good parent or loving your child. If God decided to wire your child's brain a certain way or allowed something to happen that results in your child having other issues, there is a reason and a purpose for it. Dig in, remain hopeful, and believe that He will work all things out for your good.

However, Walter's diagnosis wasn't the end: Through our journey with him, we also realized that Asher was on the spectrum, though he is higher functioning than Walter. At first, we thought Asher had Attention Deficit Disorder because he was having difficulty focusing and sitting still in class, but his test results showed Attention Deficit/Hyperactivity Disorder, Tourette syndrome, and autism.

Like Walter, today, Asher is also thriving. The Family Empowerment Scholarship has provided us with some home resources, including weighted blankets and body socks.

One thing we do as a family is post a weekly dinner menu on our refrigerator so the boys know what is coming without having to ask or stress over it. Routines are extremely helpful for kids on the spectrum. Of course, things are going to come up and schedules are going to change, but the ultimate goal is to have as many preemptive plans and conversations as possible. I also got Walter his own Garmin GPS wireless unit to hold when we drive anywhere, because he always asks, "How much further?" and "How many more minutes?" With his own GPS unit, he can follow our route and stay informed on the journey without having to ask anyone else.

When the Colombian government told us we had to move there for thirty days, I felt a lot of anxiety because of Asher and Walter's autism. Like many on the spectrum, neither of them eat a very wide variety of foods, and moving to Colombia meant we wouldn't be able to go through a McDonald's drive-through to grab some chicken nuggets and fries. We worried about what foods would be available to us there and how we would adapt to mealtimes. We had structure and routine down pat at home, but Colombia would throw all that off.

For example, let's say we're driving home and one of the boys asks, "Dad, can I get some water when we get home?" When I say yes, he responds, "Okay, can I get ice in it?" I answer yes again and then add, "You don't have to ask for ice in your water. You can have it every time." His response will be something like, "Okay, can I have five pieces of ice?" My answer again is yes. When we get home, if I give him a glass of water with four or six ice cubes in it, we'll have a problem. Because based on our conversation coming home, he is going to count the cubes. If the number is off, he is definitely going to say, "Dad, you said five."

People who don't have any experience with autistic children might say, "Well, that's just being a brat. He just needs to get over it and learn. Be grateful for water and ice." But in parenting an autistic child, you learn that it's not about any of that; the neurological disorder has everything to do with order and structure. Life is a series of math problems. The movie *The Accountant* clearly depicts this aspect of autism. Likewise, the TV series *The Good Doctor* is based on one individual with autism's amazing ability to process and apply systems and procedures. That's just the way the autistic brain is wired—very logistic and logical. Everything has to be in place. That's why many autistic adults present as absolutely brilliant people who just have some quirky and socially awkward characteristics.

For any of us, we know that numbers don't lie. They make sense. Two plus two will always and forever be four. Math is factual and provides a solvable equation with only one right answer. But that's the way a person with autism thinks about everything. Most of life is an equation. Remember, five ice cubes, not four, not six.

For me, the often-quoted Proverbs 22:6 tells us to "train up a child in the way he or she should go." For me, this has come to mean that every child needs intentional training, because we're all very different. Our perceptions and perspectives are all unique. We need to understand how to best tap into our brains and our wiring. Gaining understanding of my children's faith has been one of the most encouraging things in my own Christian walk. Seeing how Jesus has shown up in very real ways for all three of my boys, however they may struggle, has also shown me ways to help them. Their courage in facing the issues of life has been incredibly inspiring.

Settling In, Settling Down

Johana was the third of four kids in her birth family. As is very common in the Third World, her parents had to spend long hours trying to make a living, so Johana had always taken care of her younger sibling. All she knew about family was being maternal—so in many ways, her childhood had been stolen from her. Knowing this, we were able to let her go back and experience being a little girl for the first time.

The first toy she wanted was the classic Mr. Potato Head. She had never had anything like that growing up, and certainly no "little girl things." Of course, like any good brother, Asher picked on her as his older sister for playing Barbie games on her iPad and watching "silly" kids' shows. But we wanted to give her the opportunity to make up for what was lost, knowing that soon enough she would catch back up to her current age, which she did.

I loved being able to give her some of her childhood back, and the boys loved having a sister. They took her in immediately. With all three of her new brothers being younger, she stepped right into her role of big sister, which all three boys loved. Quickly, she and Henry, the youngest, became inseparable. Even in the first couple of days in Colombia, they would hold hands as we all walked down the roads. I have pictures of those early moments.

To Johana, it was like having her own younger brother back. At first, she could only talk to the boys in Spanish, so after thirty days in Colombia, all three were starting to speak Spanish to Johana as she was learning English.

Once we got past the foster crisis, God showed me that these four blessings from Him were exactly what He had planned all along—autism, ADHD, adoption, and all. He knew Johana was going to be the perfect complement to Asher, Walter, and Henry.

But right when we all thought that life was going to settle down to normal (whatever that is), we had no idea that everything—and I mean *everything*—was about to change in ways we never could have imagined.

CHAPTER FIVE

A Lazarus Experience

December 19 was Walter's seventh birthday. He was sick with the flu. Being down for the count on your big day is a bummer, especially for a kid. Friends can't come over and the all-important cake and presents have to be delayed.

But by Christmas Eve, Walter was feeling much better, and we were confident he was no longer contagious, so we decided to go ahead and attend the service at church. We took family photos in front of the huge tree that had been decorated in the lobby.

On Christmas morning, we followed our usual family tradition of letting each kid open their presents as they woke up, rather than waiting until everyone was together. But later in the day, I started feeling a bit weird.

At first, I didn't make much of it, thinking, *Huh, I wonder if I could be getting sick?* But by the morning of the twenty-sixth, I knew without a doubt I had the flu. Based on my track record, I figured I'd be down for two or three days. I would get some rest and be good to go well before New Year's.

After waking up on December 28, I was no better. My primary care doctor, like so many others during the holiday period, was unavailable, and walk-in appointments at other facilities were limited, so I decided to just drive myself to the ER.

When I arrived, I checked in and joined all the other people in the waiting room who were thinking, *I wonder how long I'm going to sit here?* Finally, I was called to an exam room. My temperature and blood pressure were checked, then I was asked several diagnostic questions to determine what was going on.

I was told I had the flu. They gave me a shot and a steroid, then told me to go home, drink plenty of fluids, and get some rest. One of the staff said to come back if I was not better in a few days.

The next morning, I woke up feeling even worse. The shots seemed to have had zero effect, so I returned to the same ER. Once again, I drove myself there and went through the check-in to wait until I was called back to an exam room. Along with my other symptoms, I told them I was also having some chest pain and shortness of breath. They said I was most likely having an allergic reaction to the shot. So they gave me a different treatment and sent me home.

Day by day, I kept getting sicker. I knew something had to be very wrong, so on New Year's Eve, I went back for the third time. The waiting room was packed, so I walked up to the triage door, opened it slightly, and stuck my head in to look around. There were several people standing there, and I could tell that a few of them recognized me.

"Hey, I'm back. I'm feeling worse," I said. "Along with everything I told you a couple of days ago, now I feel like my throat is full of glass. What do I need to do?"

I was told to go home, get some rest, and drink plenty of fluids.

So once again I drove myself back home. I realize now I probably should not have been driving.

Within a few hours, I could feel myself rapidly declining. I began to feel agitated. I couldn't sit still. As ill as I now know that I was, I can remember somehow pacing around the house. Then I started losing control of everything from my bladder to my speech. I was slurring some words and forgetting others. I peed in my pants and didn't even realize it. (Despite what many of my friends might say, no, that is not normal for me.)

My wife-at-the-time drove me back to the ER for my fourth visit. By now, in addition to losing control of every bodily function, my primary complaint was chest pains. I felt like I was having a heart attack.

When we arrived at the hospital, we told them the new details. They took one look at me, got me into a room, and immediately started running tests, hooking me up to an IV and various machines.

My next *clear* memory is waking up from a coma.

Before long, it became apparent that I was falling into multi-system organ failure from sepsis—a life-threatening blood infection that had been taking over my body for the last several days. By that point, my chances of survival were down to just 1.7 percent.

How in the world does someone come up with 1.7 as a percentage? What nerd in a cubicle somewhere was calculating numbers and decided that mine landed on 1.7? Couldn't he at least round me up to 2 percent?! It's funny to say that when telling my story now—but for my family to hear it at the time was confusing and terrifying.

Everyone knew I had been sick since Christmas but were absolutely shocked to hear that I was on the verge of death. Within a matter of hours, my situation had gone from "Go home and get some rest" to "We're minute by minute now. You need to call in the family to say goodbye."

So all my family and friends started making their way to the hospital. I wasn't expected to make it through the night.

One of my extended family members at that time worked in the medical field. On the drive to the hospital, the Lord spoke to her and said I needed to be placed on an ECMO machine.

The Mayo Clinic explains the purpose of this medical device:

> In extracorporeal membrane oxygenation (ECMO), blood is pumped outside of your body to a heart-lung machine that removes carbon dioxide and sends oxygen-filled blood back to tissues in the body. Blood flows from the right side of the heart to the membrane oxygenator in the heart-lung machine, and then is rewarmed and sent back to the body. This method allows the blood to "bypass" the heart and lungs, allowing these organs to rest and heal. . . . ECMO may be used to help people who are very ill with conditions of the heart and lung, or who are waiting for or recovering from a heart transplant. It may be an option when other life support measures haven't worked.[1]

1 Mayo Clinic Staff, "Extracorporeal Membrane Oxygenation (ECMO)," Mayo Clinic, April 19, 2022, https://www.mayoclinic.org/tests-procedures/ecmo/about/pac-20484615.

When the family member arrived at the hospital and saw my condition, the word from the Lord was confirmed and they gathered the doctors and nurses. The request was made, along with the reasoning as to why this would be a viable option. At the time, only seven hospitals in Florida had ECMO machines, and this wasn't one of them. Knowing they were at the end of their rope, the staff offered to work out a transfer anywhere my family wanted to send me.

The best option was a hospital in Orlando, and the staff lost no time making arrangements for the transfer. But the actual process of transport takes a while, especially on a holiday. Ordering a Life Flight helicopter is not like getting an Uber. The staff switched me over to portable life-support machines, then wheeled me to a waiting area closer to the exit door that led to the helipad.

Soon, the helicopter appeared in the distance. As the pilot slowed down over his target, he began to hover and start the descent. But then suddenly he shot right back up into the air and disappeared over the horizon within seconds.

I was literally dying. Why would the helicopter show up and then leave when we were right there, waiting?

To my family, this seemed cruel. They demanded answers and were eventually told the dispatcher had informed the pilot to leave and go to an accident that was deemed to be priority. I guess someone more important was dying faster than I was? While the explanation made sense to all the first responders because that's the world they live in every day, my family just felt helpless. The staff assured them that a Life Flight would be sent as soon as one was available. But by now, a very long hour had already passed, and my life was hanging by a thread.

Finally, they told my family that a helicopter was definitely on its way. Once it landed and I was loaded on, we flew thirty minutes to Orlando's Advent Hospital and I was taken straight to the intensive care unit. Bottom line—on December 31, 2019, around the time the rest of the world was shouting "Happy New Year!" I was in the biggest fight of my life.

When my family arrived and found my room, the ICU staff began to understand how dire my condition actually was.

"Why is he here?" one of them asked. "Why was he brought here? There's nothing we can do for him."

When my family explained I needed an ECMO machine, one of the doctors said I wasn't a candidate for it because I wasn't a heart or lung transplant patient. Technically, he was right.

The staff hooked me up to every life support machine they had but told my family what everyone knows is the precursory medical statement to impending death: "We'll make him as comfortable as possible."

But something was about to happen that would change the game.

Time of Death

At most hospitals, shift changes take place at 7:00 p.m. and 7:00 a.m. The first thing the new round of doctors and nurses do is survey the patients and get a handle on their needs.

At 7:18 a.m. on January 1, 2020, just as the new shift came into my room, every single machine connected to me went off simultaneously—all of them emitting those long, ear-piercing beeps you hear on TV shows when the patient "codes."

That's the moment when, for all intents and purposes, I died. I had no pulse and was not breathing.

I was told that within thirty seconds, my entire body started to turn blue. A nurse jumped up onto the bed and started compressions to try to bring me back. The rest of the team launched into all their life-saving protocols.

But my body was not responding. After ten minutes of compressions and doing everything they were trained to do, the doctors and nurses were losing hope. At 7:29 a.m.—eleven minutes later—one of the nurses checked me one last time before stopping the protocols. To her amazement, she detected a very faint pulse. She called out, "We got a pulse! We got a pulse!" At that point, the ER staff continued to do everything possible to bring my vitals back up.

Somehow, I was alive.

So, did I really die? Well, even though a doctor had not yet officially declared me dead when all the life-saving measures were clearly not working, from 7:18 to 7:29 a.m., I had no pulse and was not breathing. I didn't have any sort of out-of-body experience. I didn't float up into a corner of the room to watch what was going on or see a bright light from Heaven and the outline of Jesus walking toward me. There was nothing like that.

If you're wondering how I didn't sustain any brain damage from all that, remember, they didn't turn off any of the machines. My brain was never deprived of oxygen.

The Hail Mary Experience

Dr. Linda Bogar, a cardiothoracic surgeon who dealt with heart and lung transplants at the hospital, had just seen her last patient after being on call for the night. She was the doctor who could decide to put someone on an ECMO machine. Not until months later did we discover that Dr. Bogar, being a Christian, had felt a prompting to hang around the hospital for a while instead of going home at 7:00 a.m.

Once I had pulled through, the main ER doctor found out Dr. Bogar was still on her floor and asked her, "Would you come down and evaluate a young man who just coded, but came back? His family has requested that he be considered as a potential ECMO candidate."

While the initial information didn't sound promising to her, she knew she had felt the need to stay at work for some reason. So she agreed to take a look at me.

There are certain criteria that add up to a score used to decide who goes on ECMO and who doesn't; hospitals need to steward their resources, so they don't want to use something as drastic as an ECMO machine only to prolong the inevitable. But Dr. Bogar didn't calculate my score. When the ER doctor told her I had less than a 50 percent chance of survival and was not a transplant patient, she was skeptical. And after going to the ER, listening to the doctor, looking at the data, and seeing my condition, Dr. Bogar's answer was no. She didn't feel like I was a good candidate.

The ER doctor offered to take Dr. Bogar out to the waiting room and introduce her to my family and friends. Someone had to give them her assessment. She was surprised by the number of people gathered there—not just the usual two or three family members, but a large group that obviously cared about me, several of whom were crying and visibly upset.

And they all begged Dr. Bogar to help me any way she could—specifically to put me on the ECMO machine. She was touched by the love and care everyone in the waiting room had for me. As she listened, all the while knowing she had stayed at the hospital for a reason, miraculously, she changed her mind.

"Okay," she told them, "we're still minute by minute with Gary, but we're going to throw a 'hail Mary' and put him on the ECMO machine."

Because the hospital wasn't at capacity—or over it, as it would be a few months later when the COVID-19 pandemic struck—she was able to take that risk. As it turned out, ECMO machines were about to be in incredibly high demand with a very low supply around the entire nation.

Even so, Dr. Bogar was very clear with my friends and family that this approach might not work: If I didn't start to turn around after a few days, or if there were any complications at all, she would have to turn the machine off. My family said they were willing to accept the risk and move forward. To them, this was the only reason they had requested I be transferred to that hospital.

The doctors immediately took me to the operating room where they inserted two lines—running from each side of my groin up to my heart—and attached them to the ECMO. Thank God, everything went smoothly and there were no issues. Next, they took me to a different intensive care unit in the hospital to begin monitoring my progress.

The word my relative had heard from God finally made sense. If the helicopter had not been delayed and I had arrived when it seemed like I was "supposed to," Dr. Bogar still would have been with other patients—proving once again that when God is involved, there is no such thing as early or late, only right on time. He had orchestrated everything right down to the minute.

Dr. Bogar stayed close to my room and, once she saw that I was doing as well as could be expected, she went home after a very long night and morning. While everyone on the intensive care staff was doing all they could, it was still very challenging to keep my blood pressure up—and me alive.

On her shift at Advent, Dr. Bogar went to my room to check on my status and saw my entire family gathered around my bed. There was always Christian music playing softly in the room. Often, someone would set their phone by my ear, hoping the songs would inspire me to hang on and fight.

As Dr. Bogar slipped into my room to check the ECMO machine, she politely asked about the choice of music. When someone answered that band playing was MercyMe, the doctor said, "Yes, I know those songs. I listen to Christian radio, and they have always been one of my favorite artists." My family then told her about my connection to the band and how we have been friends for many years.

Later, Dr. Bogar told me, "That day I came into your room, I thought about what a wonderful picture this was, with your family and the music creating a support system of faith. I felt a sense of peace in your room, which made me think there was hope for you after all. But even with that, as a doctor, I knew that if you did pull through, your limbs were going to be a problem."

Dr. Bogar had a lot of experience with heart and lung transplant patients on the ECMO machine, and she was absolutely right. Over the next several days, while my core was slowly gaining strength, my limbs continued to get worse. While my vital organs were being kept alive, my arms and legs weren't receiving their usual supply of oxygenated blood and, as a result, all four limbs started dying. My fingers and toes began to turn black and become rock-hard. Then my hands and feet. Then my ankles and wrists.

Most people aren't on ECMO for very long. But I was on it for ten days.

The next time Dr. Bogar came to check on me, I was waking up and the staff was starting to scale back some of my medications. She saw I had taken a turn for the better and would likely survive. She had discussed with my family the risk of me losing limbs, but they all agreed to keep going with the ECMO. Their consensus was, "As long as he's alive, however he comes out of this, it's okay."

Dr. Bogar told me, "All of us who had seen how far you had come knew what a miracle this was."

Every photo taken in that time frame shows somebody standing beside my bed, praying over me. I was never alone. From what I was told and could see, the prayers were intense and constant. While I can't remember hearing anything, I am sure my spirit picked up every word prayed on my behalf.

A New Voice

On January 10, I came out of the coma. The first thing I saw when I cracked my eyes open was my mom's face right in front of me—almost nose to nose. It was a bit weird to wake up and see her that close. I had no idea what was going on, why I was there, what was happening, or any of the problems with my body.

Once I became coherent, I started to learn the gravity of my situation.

The doctors explained two medical terms to me. The first was "necrotic," meaning my muscles and tissues were dying. The second was "mummified," which means they were rotting, shriveling up, and drying out. Once anything is mummified, it is past the point of no return.

At that point, the conversation included a new term: amputation.

Making matters worse was the fact that I had no ability to speak for nearly two weeks after emerging from the coma. I tried, but nothing would come out of my mouth. I got good enough at mouthing words to communicate simple messages—like "hot," "cold," "thirsty," or "hungry."

Finally, the doctor decided to perform a tracheotomy to see if that might affect my speech. They made an incision in my throat and ran a tube in to see if that might give me my voice back. Somehow, it worked. Within seconds of them placing the trach tube, my voice returned, and I was able to speak again. That felt miraculous to me.

The tube stayed in for the next few weeks, until whatever damage that had rendered me unable to speak was healed. When the tube came out, even though I had a giant hole in my neck, my voice remained. The incision took three or four more days to close up. We had to stay on high alert, because any time I would eat, drink, or cough, "stuff" would come out of the hole. That was awful and very gross. I was grateful when the incision finally closed.

This strange vocal condition during my hospital stay became the inspiration for my new career as a Christian communicator and motivational speaker. My inability to communicate was the reason I chose "Gary Miracle Speaks." There were three times when I couldn't speak. The first was when I died. The second was when I was revived, but remained in a coma, and the third was after I woke up and physically couldn't speak. My logo is a screenshot of my flat line and then the slight pulse when I came back. The EKG line is actually from when I was dead. Then at the first beat of my heart at 7:29 a.m. I have the actual record with the doctor's handwriting. Those few minutes will always be amazing to me. I believe I was given my life back for a reason. I now have a responsibility to use my restored and revived voice to speak of the redemption and righteousness available through Jesus Christ.

A Best Friend's Goodbye

One of the strangest things that happened to me in the hospital involved my dog of ten years, Bones.

The day I woke up from the coma, I was moved to my own room on the ICU floor. I felt like I was in a dungeon with concrete walls and no windows. With all the machines constantly beeping, the experience was awful. My family was there, but as I told you, I couldn't speak.

I vividly remember looking to my right at one point and seeing Bones there in a chair next to my bed. I recall thinking how strange it was that the staff had allowed him into the hospital. I started trying to mouth the words to ask, "Why is Bones here? What's he doing in here?" Once my family finally realized what I was trying to say, they assumed I was delirious and still under the effects of the coma. They kept insisting that Bones wasn't there. But when I looked over at the chair, there he was. I knew I wasn't crazy, delirious, or hallucinating. It was all so real.

While I was arguing with my family about all this, Bones jumped off the chair and walked across the hall into another patient's room—an older man. Concerned that he was going to bother someone and get kicked out, I finally convinced someone to go across the hall and get Bones. If the hospital staff had been gracious enough to allow him in to see me, then I needed to keep him in my room.

My family decided to humor me. I watched as someone walked over to the other patient's room, looked around, and came back. I looked over at the chair next to the bed, and there was Bones, sitting there and looking at me. A few minutes later, I looked over again and he was gone. I didn't see him again after that.

About six weeks later, while I was still in the hospital, my family said they had some bad news: The day I woke up from the coma, Bones had died.

While that made me sad, it also made sense: I believe my dog came to say goodbye to me in the hospital. It was as if he waited for me to wake up from my coma so he could tell me goodbye. Once I was awake, he could let go.

I can see why some people—especially those who don't consider themselves "animal people"—would roll their eyes and refuse to believe that, spiritually, something like that could happen. But to me, that experience isn't really about me or my dog, but about the God who cares about the details of our lives. I believe He allowed me to have closure with a faithful friend who had been there for me through thick and thin for an entire decade.

The Takeaway from the Giver

Finally, the doctors had "the talk" with me about the reality of four amputations—both arms and both legs.

I am not now, nor have I ever been, some kind of super-Christian. I've never been good at giving Sunday school answers about faith or the guy who spits out Christian bumper sticker clichés. When I heard I was going to lose all four of my limbs, the only thing I could think of was Job 1:21.

> "Naked I came from my mother's womb, and naked I will depart. The LORD gave and the Lord has taken away; may the name of the LORD be praised." (NIV)

But I thought about it in the present tense, "The Lord gives and the Lord takes away." Through everything that has happened to me, there is one thing I now know for sure: Throughout my life, the Lord has given me everything I've ever needed. Up to that point, I had been living the American Dream with the all-American family. He had given me everything I needed and a lot that I didn't, along with many things I just wanted. But I hadn't done any of that myself; it all came from His hand.

I once heard pastor and author Craig Groeschel speak at a Catalyst Conference about this, asking the crowd, "When something bad happens, will we still say that God is good?" At that point, I began to realize that throughout my entire life, I had grown accustomed to God only giving. I didn't consider the fact that He also has the right to take away. In our Western culture, we seem to always ask, *Why would a good God "take away"?*

That mindset is not only wrong, it's unbiblical. In fact, I often think that when we do experience a "take away" situation, the enemy comes along and whispers things like, "If God really loved you, this would not have happened," or "What great sin did you commit that caused Him to allow this in your life?" All of those lies are designed to keep us from the last part of the verse: "May the name of the Lord be praised." That is the real point of the scripture—not God's giving or taking, but the fact that, regardless of what happens in life, He deserves our praise.

I realized I was extremely thankful when the Lord gave, but I'd never known what it truly meant for Him to take away. In that moment of revelation, an overwhelming peace washed over me. With everything the Lord had given me all my life, I had a peace that it was time for Him to take away my hands and feet, my arms and legs.

Up until that point throughout my Christian life, I had always said, "God is good." And I believed it. But typically, I said it right after something good had happened to me. I had even preached about God's goodness in relation to His blessings. But what was I going to do now that something extremely traumatic had happened in my life? Was I going to live like God is no longer good? Or was I going to spend my life saying that He is good? Preaching that He is good? And trying to convince other people to believe that, too?

After losing all his children and being struck with a horrible disease, Job said of God, "Though he slay me, I will hope in him" (Job 13:15 ESV). With everything I was facing now, would I choose the same attitude?

CHAPTER SIX

Jesus (Still) Saves

For the entire three and a half months I spent in the hospital, my family and friends created an around-the-clock schedule, ensuring I was never left alone for longer than five minutes, day or night. Just as the nurses clocked in and out, so did the volunteer community that surrounded me with love.

On February 2, 2020— the day the Kansas City Chiefs beat the San Francisco 49ers in Super Bowl LIV—my buddy Joe was by my side for his weekly Sunday day shift. Of course, he and I were watching the big game together on the not-so-big-screen TV mounted on the wall of my hospital room. The plan that day was for him to stay into the evening until the end of the game, longer than he usually did, then hand me off to my mom for the night shift.

Mom showed up about twenty minutes before the game was over. At the final whistle, the Chiefs had beaten the Niners 31–20. Joe gave me a hug and left.

About five minutes later, I began struggling to breathe. Mom ran into the hallway and shouted for the doctors and nurses to come. All the call buttons were hit, and a nurse got on the intercom, calling for the staff to get to my room. Out of nowhere, I was going down again, and nobody knew why. They even brought in a crash cart.

The entire crisis lasted about thirty minutes, but it felt like hours. The team finally got me stabilized, and afterward I appeared to be back to normal. The unnerving part is that no one was able to figure out why that happened. As a lifelong Dallas Cowboys fan, I guess I must have just been really upset that the AFC team won the game.

Under the Knife, Literally

Shortly after my doctors had the amputation discussion with me and my family, the vascular surgeons recommended we do the surgeries as soon as possible. I don't want to project this onto all surgeons, but I don't think this group was terribly concerned about what my life would look like down the road. They saw the inevitability of my situation and were ready to do their job—which, to be blunt, was to cut my limbs off as neatly and precisely as possible.

But for quite a while, we told them, "We're going to let God make that decision, not you. We want to wait as long as we can and hope for healing." We had that conversation several times, until they finally agreed to allow us to wait. But they always closed with a clear warning, saying, "Okay, but at the slightest sign of infection, it's going to turn into an emergency amputation, because your body can't take another round of septic shock. You won't be able to fight that off again."

As I mentioned earlier, I had already gotten a peace about *what* had to happen. But I didn't have a peace about *when* yet. As far as I was concerned, on any given day I could say the word and my limbs would be gone. Once they were, that would be it and I couldn't reverse it—so I was going to wait. We remained on high alert for any sign of an infection, such as a clear change in the skin or a strange odor. Both are bad signs.

About two months later, the worst happened: Infection started to set in on one of my hands. My doctors said they'd let me keep my legs—for now—but it was time not only to take that one hand, but *both,* in order to save my elbows. An amputee's quality of life is much better with the joints intact than without them. Without joints, prosthetic limbs must be created using hydraulics, which, while possible, is just more involved and creates a more difficult experience than when you have joints of your own.

In researching amputation and prosthetics, my family had found it helps to include a plastic surgeon in the process. As specialists, they can reroute specific nerve endings to avoid any residual phantom pains—a common phenomenon in which amputees still feel their missing limbs. Those sensations can create a great deal of pain.

My plastic surgeon, Dr. Patel, was a miracle worker. (No pun intended. Okay, maybe a little. It's uncommon for plastic surgeons to be involved in lower-extremity amputations. We had to jump through several hoops and get a *lot* of approvals from a *lot* of people in a *lot* of places to allow him to be part of all four of my amputations.

But the inevitable day finally came. On March 18, 2020, the surgeons amputated both my arms, up to just below the elbows. Thankfully, with Dr. Patel's help, everything went perfectly; the wounds stayed clean and closed nicely. The way I saw it, the Lord took my hands. He allowed me to have them for almost four decades, but from that point until I reach Heaven, He will help me manage life without them. And, with another nod to both the Lord and Dr. Patel, I have never experienced any phantom pains.

About a week later, I was lying in my hospital bed, talking to a few of the nurses, when someone came in to change my bandages. By that point, the skin on my left leg was so necrotic that it wasn't strong enough to hold my muscles and tendons inside. When the bandage was removed, they literally fell out of my calf. Everything below my knee was coming apart, so they started prepping me for emergency surgery—the amputation of my left leg.

Before wheeling me out, the surgeons gave me the now-familiar warning: They wouldn't know if they could save my left knee until they got in there and could see what they were working with. My last thought as I went under anesthesia was wondering if I would wake up with my knee—or not.

I will never forget opening my eyes in the recovery room. I was all alone and trying to shake off the grogginess. My last thought from before came rushing back to the front of my brain. I lay there, staring at the ceiling, scared to death to look down for what felt like hours but was likely just a few minutes. Finally, I prayed for the strength to look and accept whatever I saw. I quickly glanced down and there was my knee!

I. Was. Ecstatic!

As I lay there, thanking God over and over for preserving my knee, the surgeons came in to tell me that, just as with my arms, everything had gone perfectly. That wound also closed up nicely with no issues. So, on March 28, 2020, the Lord decided that it was time to take my leg.

I had now lost three out of four limbs and knew losing the fourth was just a matter of time. But under the circumstances, I was doing well mentally and emotionally.

On the morning of April 1, my doctors surprised me by saying they were going to discharge me to go home—with my right leg intact. They had made arrangements for an in-home health care nurse to keep an eye on my leg and watch out for infection.

Since it was April Fools' Day and the whole staff knew by now I was a comedian, at first, I thought this might be just a well-orchestrated joke. But I soon saw the seriousness on their faces and realized this was for real.

I was going home. Finally.

Where Did Everybody Go?

When I was wheeled out of my room into the hallway leading to the hospital exit, I turned the corner to find all the doctors and nurses lining the hall, clapping and cheering. While I understand why they chose to celebrate my discharge that way, I knew I was the one who needed to be clapping and cheering for all of them—if I could. These people had saved my life and served me well for 107 days. True medical professionals who see their career not just as a job but as a calling are amazing people, and I had the privilege of getting to know many of them in my time there.

The paramedics took me outside into the light of day for the first time since December, pushing my gurney into the ambulance to transport me from Orlando back home. That drive was a surreal experience, one I will never forget. By that point, the COVID-19 pandemic was in full force, and looking out the windows at the empty streets made me feel like we were driving through the apocalypse.

My family hadn't talked much about COVID with me, so I didn't fully understand. I didn't know where everybody was. Because I binge-watched Netflix all day in the hospital instead of watching the news, I was severely out of touch with reality.

One of my kids had gotten sick at some point, so the rest of the family was at someone else's house, stuck in quarantine—so the paramedics wheeled me inside and transferred me to my bed. I knew that keeping me from being exposed to anything, especially while my leg continued to heal, was the right move. Even still, coming home to an empty house, with the world shut down and my family gone, was extremely depressing. I felt like I had been sent into a black hole. The flu had almost killed me, but nothing had ever shut the whole world down before. Throughout the next week, I got a crash course in everything that was happening in the world.

I had no idea how hard life was about to become. Once my kids got back, I started to feel a level of humiliation I had never experienced before. Of course, that had nothing to do with them or how they responded to me; it was just my own pride as a man and how I assumed they must view me in my condition.

For example, I had to be moved around my own home by a Hoyer Lift, a giant blue blanket suspended on all four corners by a massive hook. I would roll over onto my side, my family would lower the blanket onto the bed, and then I would roll onto it. Then someone would operate the lift to pick me up and take me wherever I needed to go.

So, there I was, helplessly dangling in this hammock like a captured zoo animal, with my kids wheeling me out of my room and dropping me on the couch so I could lie there and watch TV with them. I was embarrassed about all the things I could no longer do.

But the most incredible thing I eventually came to understand was that my kids did *not* see me the way I saw myself. They turned a blind eye to how I looked and saw what I was going through. All they wanted to do was help their dad.

One of the most beautiful ways I experienced this was through Johana feeding me *every* single meal. Meanwhile my three boys thought it was the greatest thing in the world to wheel me around the house in the Hoyer Lift. I cried a lot of tears from being humbled in front of my kids, but they were having the time of their lives serving me.

It's interesting to realize how we humans can see the same thing in such different ways. I felt a ton of pressure that my kids didn't feel at all. They were just excited that Dad was home. At first, I wasted valuable time throwing a pity party when I could have been hanging out and having fun, too. That was a tough process I had to work through—but then came the pivotal day when I drew a line in the sand for myself.

I had to ask myself some tough questions. *Am I going to sit here on the couch, get addicted to pain pills, and just watch life go by without me? Or am I going to take joy in this new journey and fight like crazy to figure out how to do life on this side of what has happened to me? Am I just going to waste my life because I'm so bummed about what's happened to me that I'm not going to be able to walk my daughter down the aisle someday?! No way! That is not going to happen!*

I knew the proverbial elephant had to be eaten one very small bite at a time, so I decided to tackle a previously menial task each day. The first one was trying to charge my cell phone. You don't even have to think about doing that; it's muscle memory. You see the battery is low and within a second, you plug it in. But imagine having only blunt stumps where your hands used to be.

I knew the end of my phone cable was lying on my nightstand, already plugged into the outlet. I rolled into the bedroom with my phone in my lap, stared at the end of the cable, then began trying to pick it up with my stumps. After pouring sweat, crying hard, screaming in a fit of the greatest frustration I had ever felt, and biting into a pillow, three—yes, three—hours later, I managed to get it done.

Something that had once taken me a fraction of a second to do now took three hours. I felt worthless and helpless. I no longer even felt like a man. It was like Satan was whispering in my ear, making sure I understood all the things I couldn't do anymore. I heard, *Just give up. This is useless. Life isn't worth it. It's over for you. You're no good to anyone anymore.* The worst part was that it was really hard for me to disagree with him. Those thoughts were just leveraging what I felt about myself.

The next day I decided to try putting laundry into the washing machine, piece by piece. The day after that, I took the garbage outside and put it in the trash can. I kept thinking about all the important life events I wanted to take part in one day with my kids, so I just kept practicing and practicing and practicing the little things.

Today, I can grab a cable and plug in my phone as fast as I could before. I was learning what I had to do not just to survive, but to live.

A One-in-Twelve Shot

On April 22, I noticed an odor coming from my right leg. I knew what that meant: infection was setting in on my last limb.

Then it began to get that unusual look as well, so we decided to go get it checked out. My doctor confirmed that we needed to take it off.

So on April 25, I returned to the hospital for my final amputation. Once again, there was no way to tell whether the surgeons could save my knee until the operation was under way. Once again, I was filled with fear and tension.

Like Bill Murray in *Groundhog Day*, I woke up from the anesthesia in the recovery room alone, afraid to look down and see if I had my knee or not. I stared at the ceiling, trying to muster up the courage. But when I finally did look, there was my knee! It matched my other leg!

I was just as ecstatic on April 25 as I had been on March 28; with my final limb removed, I still had all my joints! Prosthetics were possible. I might hold things someday. I might be able to walk someday.

This time, however, my surgeons also had some potential bad news: There was an area on the inside of my leg where they couldn't close the skin all the way over my stump. It was so necrotic and mummified that every time they tried to staple or stitch it shut, the closures wouldn't hold.

I had three options: The first was to hope that the skin would close on its own and heal. The second would be an additional operation called a wound vac, a type of therapy that promotes healing and prevents infection. The third option was to amputate even more of my leg, most likely above the knee, if the infection got worse.

Obviously, that news was very stressful. My anxiety went through the roof. In addition to being able to look straight into the giant open wound on the side of my leg, I had to live with more questions of what might be taken away.

I prayed constantly for God to heal me. After all the antibiotics I'd been on during my long hospital stay, my body had become virtually resistant to any of them. Even so, I was sent home with a super-strong antibiotic, but it just made me throw up all day. I still had a central line attached that could send any medication in through my arm, all the way up through my collarbone, and back down to my heart. My in-home nurse came every day to check my vitals, administer anything I needed, and keep the bandages changed and applied correctly.

On the Thursday before Mother's Day weekend, when the nurse arrived, she checked my leg and said, "Oh, my goodness. This does *not* look good. We need to go get this checked out." We went straight to my vascular surgeon, who took some swabs to get cultures on the tissue. I then returned home to await the results.

Every Friday after my discharge, Dad would bring over lunch and we would eat together. On this particular Friday, we were eating Whoppers from Burger King when the doctor called with the results: I had a staph infection in the wound—the worst possible scenario.

I hung up the phone and broke down crying. Dad didn't even ask me what had been said, because he knew. He just came over and wrapped me in a huge dad hug.

I knew this likely meant I would face an above-the-knee amputation to get rid of the infected tissue. Within the hour—kicking and screaming inside—I was back at the hospital. When we arrived, the infectious disease doctor who had been with me for my entire 107-day stay was on call. Knowing better than anyone what I was up against, he surprised me by saying that we had a one-in-twelve shot of finding a different antibiotic that might prevent further amputation.

This was yet another miracle God brought about for me, in two parts: The first was that this doctor cared enough to take the time to help me, and the second was the final result. With twelve possible drugs to choose from, but only having enough borrowed time to try one, he made the decision and sent me home with the specific antibiotic to be injected through my central line.

In short, he nailed it. He reviewed my entire history and picked the one medication that could heal the infection and the wound.

There was also a downside: The antibiotic was so potent that it left me either throwing up or dry heaving 24/7 for the next four or five days. But, as hard as that week was, anything was better than living the rest of my life without the knee joint on my right leg.

The infection did heal and the skin flap on my leg closed. From there, I never looked back. I began to work out and have regular sessions with an occupational therapist. A pharmacist helped me get my first motorized wheelchair. I was starting to find my new normal.

At Just the Right Time

Walking through my entire story from the first day of the sickness to getting home after all my amputations, the number of miracles is mind-blowing. Going from a 1.7 percent chance of living to dying to being in a coma for ten days, but coming back. Not being able to talk for ten days, then the trach tube placed, allowing me to speak. My crash right after the Super Bowl, but coming back. The one correct antibiotic being chosen to save my knee. All four amputations done without losing my joints.

There's another miracle I haven't shared with you yet. Early on, when things were still touch-and-go, I was hooked up to a lot of machines. My family and friends were told that one of the readings was 40, but it needed to be at 100. That was the crisis of the moment. Everyone stood around my bed, and someone placed some anointing oil on my forehead. Then they all began to pray for God to intervene in my body and change the number. By the time the last person prayed, they looked at that monitor and it read "100." Those were such visual moments for all of us to see God show up and experience Him in ways that I didn't even know were possible prior to this illness.

So many times, Jesus showed up to save me. I 100 percent believe He saved me as a preteen. I 100 percent believe He got my attention and walked me through what it meant for Him to be the Lord of my life when I changed jobs. I 100 percent believe He led Bart to walk me through a grace transformation. Then there were the countless daily saves in the hospital to keep me alive. That means Jesus is not just Savior *once*—He keeps on being the Savior. It's not just what He does, it's who He is! The old cliché "Jesus saves" is true! He does save, and *always* in the present tense.

CHAPTER SEVEN

Say I Won't

In June, I was able to trade in my manual wheelchair for a motorized model, but learning how to drive it was tricky. Our home, like most, was not built with wheelchairs in mind, so I was constantly banging into walls and doors. I'm sure those first few weeks, I looked like I was playing bumper cars. I tried to gain more independence by, for example, motoring into the kitchen late at night to get a cup of water. I practiced those types of normal activities to try to become more self-sufficient. Eventually, we started modifying the house to create more room for me to maneuver.

Early on, I was encouraged to join some Facebook groups of amputees for peer support. I participated for a while, but soon left. The overall tone of those groups was too dark and depressing for me. People were constantly posting pictures of their wounds and stumps. They complained about their pain and talked about all the medications they were on. Some were openly confessing their opioid addiction and everything it took just to stay alive. No offense to the people in any of those groups, but personally, I just couldn't live in that space—mentally, emotionally, or spiritually. I needed hope more than I needed empathy.

But the groups did serve one very important purpose: They motivated me to get off the pain pills as fast as I could. With four kids in my house, I didn't want opioids anywhere near them. Even though I kept mine out of sight, I was nervous about one of my kids accidentally getting hold of a pill. Also, I didn't want my children to have a dad who just lay on the couch, staring at a TV all day, numbed out of his mind. I always want to set an example of what it means to be an overcomer.

I knew I was going to have to fight hard to figure out what God had planned for me from the day He first started to "knit me together in my mother's womb," as Psalm 139 states. I also realized other promises in God's Word don't contain exclusions like "unless you're an amputee." In Jeremiah 29:11, He said His plans were to "prosper" me and "not to harm" me, to give me "a hope and a future." I needed to trust that His plan was coming to pass.

My occupational therapist had me doing exercises like bicep curls by placing an empty weight bar inside my arms at the elbows. He would also have me roll a small tennis ball covered in rubber spikes between my stumps with the goal of not dropping it. All the while, I was pushing and squeezing the ball as hard as I could. This exercise had two purposes: to help get my range of motion back in my arms and to desensitize the ends of my stumps, which were still very raw and sensitive. My arms and legs had to be toughened up to stop the pain. It's hard to wrap your brain around the fact that you have to intentionally hurt yourself so that you won't unintentionally hurt yourself later!

Because the exercises were so difficult and painful, at first I could only handle about ten seconds at a time. By that point, I was down to one pain medication, only for the rehab exercises. But towards the end of July, I took my last pain pill, which was a huge step in the right direction for me. I refused to become another statistic!

How Are You Not Dead?!

In August 2020, as school was getting ready to start, my boys started getting ready for their sports teams to ramp up again. I had always been their soccer and football coach since Asher was four; now, at age ten, he was beginning to talk about trying out for a competitive soccer league. I had never coached at that level and didn't have the desire to; I was the dad who just wanted to be with my kids, and if that meant coaching, then that's what I would do. Sign me up!

Before I took Asher to the tryout, I knew that I needed to have a difficult but honest talk with him. We sat down and I cautiously asked, "Do you care if I come watch you?" I had no idea what he might say.

He looked surprised and answered, "Well, of course. Why would you not come watch me?"

"Well, I don't want to embarrass you," I said. "I wouldn't want people to tease you about the way your dad looks or that your dad's in a wheelchair or talk behind your back."

Asher's response warmed my heart.

"I couldn't care less, Dad. You *have* to be out there."

That moment was a huge motivator for me, because at that time, I was my own worst enemy. I was ashamed of how I looked. I was insecure and didn't want people to see my scars. I didn't want the side-eyes or stares. I didn't want people to pull their kids in closer to them when I passed by in my wheelchair. I had already imagined all those things and more were going to happen all the time. I projected my fears onto everyone and assumed they would look at me with pity at best—or judgment at worst.

Look at that last paragraph again. Do you see how many sentences start with "I"? That was the first problem with my mindset.

At Asher's practices, just as we had discussed, I was "out there." And I hated every second of it, because I was dealing with so many toxic thoughts about myself and fears about all the other parents. For the first time in my life, I hated watching my son play sports because I was nervous about what people were thinking and saying about me.

But that became yet another line-in-the-sand moment, as I was forced to confront myself. *Alright, Gary, what's it going to be? Are you going to keep faking and pretending, or are you going to just own it?* I had to come to grips with the cold, hard fact that there was absolutely nothing I could do about how I looked. This was my life now, and I had to choose to live it like the old hymn says, "Just As I Am."

While this may sound incredibly cheesy to some folks, one of the biggest motivators I found to press on came when I watched *The Greatest Showman*, the musical about the legendary circus icon P. T. Barnum—specifically, when the circus performers sang "This Is Me." Somehow, watching a scene about people that society considered "freaks" unapologetically celebrating their uniqueness gave me a shot of courage. (Yes, I love musicals, okay? I always have. I don't know why. And now I have gone public with that guilty pleasure.)

I decided I was not going to hide my appearance anymore. I would let anyone, anywhere stare at me anytime they wanted. I was going to go for it. So on all my social media, I posted a full-body picture of me without my bandages that showed all my open wounds and every scar. Everything. All of it. *This is me.* I also quoted some of the brilliant lyrics from the song.

Ironically, after that post, the seven degrees of separation principle kicked in.

One of my childhood friends had moved to Los Angeles and by that point had been an animator for Disney for years. Along the way, he had become friends with Keala Settle, the actress who played the bearded lady and sang the lead on "This Is Me" in the movie. She commented on my Instagram post, and we chatted there for a bit. Then we set up a FaceTime call because Keala wanted to encourage me. That was an unexpected, huge blessing I never imagined might happen. The entire experience was a major confidence booster at the perfect time.

Through a GoFundMe page we had set up at the time, I was able to purchase a minivan that could accommodate a wheelchair. That allowed me to go to every one of Asher's soccer practices and games.

When the competitive season ended, recreational season started with rec soccer and rec flag football. I had coached both sports in that league previously. Our community has a massive youth sports complex for baseball, soccer, and football, with multiple fields for each sport. Every field is covered in extremely expensive Astroturf, and as a result, the complex has a lot of rules like "no lawn chairs" and "no pets"—nothing that might damage the turf. Knowing this, I assumed there was no way they were going to allow my two-hundred-pound body on my four-hundred-pound wheelchair to get anywhere near those fields.

But with my new shot of confidence still in play, I decided to give it a go.

I emailed the commissioner, who knew me, and told him about my dilemma. He responded that he didn't know the solution but would take it to the board of directors.

To my surprise, the board approved my request—but had to get permission from the city because it's a municipal facility. Soon, I got a phone call giving me access to the fields.

So, still brimming with confidence, I took it a step further and reached out to the soccer league and football league to ask if any coaching spots were still open. The Space Coast United Soccer League president said, "Hey, Gary, we definitely want you back. But also, we want to subsidize your kids to play soccer here. Keep us informed about their sizes for cleats, uniforms, jerseys, balls, anything you need, and we'll take care of it."

I had no idea what a huge blessing one simple email would bring. From "Can I go on your field?" to "Can I coach again?" to my kids receiving a free pass to play soccer. Before long, I was back out in the field, coaching my kids—without financial stress. It was a beautiful gesture from the folks in our community.

There was just one roadblock: Even though I had coached before, a new background check was required, and that included running my fingerprints. But because I no longer had fingers, this obviously couldn't be done! The city administrators didn't know what to do, even though I offered retina scans, saliva tests, hair samples, anything I could think of as a replacement.

Finally, I stated, "There's just no way in the entire state of Florida that this is the first time you've run into this kind of issue!"

"Yes, Gary, evidently it is," they said.

Finally, my prosthetics provider reached out to a congressman, U.S. Rep. Brian Mast, who is a fellow amputee. Mast called the city, and within a few hours, they informed me we were good to go. I didn't ask any questions, I just said, "Great! Thanks!"

Regardless of how far I had come, I was still nervous when players were assigned to my team. I began to struggle with anxiety about the moment when the parents would show up with their kids and see me in my wheelchair. I imagined them saying, "Oh my gosh! How can a guy who has no legs coach soccer?!" I was about to take the old coaching joke one step farther than it had ever been before: "Those who can, do, and those who can't, coach." I certainly couldn't play, but I could coach!

So I introduced myself to all the parents via a group text message before the first practice. I gave a brief version of my story, so there would be no surprises. I let them know they would not hurt my feelings if they wanted their kids to be placed on a different team; they had my full permission, with no judgment from me. I also sent a picture of myself, so there would be no mystery about what I looked like. I also told them that on the first night of practice, I was going to spend the first thirty minutes letting the kids look at me, stare, say anything, ask questions—whatever they needed. I invited the parents to do the same. I wanted everyone on my team to feel comfortable and have fun.

At the first practice, my imagined thirty-minute orientation turned into about five minutes. My condition just wasn't the issue I thought it might be.

The best story involves a six-year-old kid on my football team who was on the autism spectrum, like two of my boys. Starting the first night, he would grab one of my arms, look at me with a puzzled expression, and ask, "How are you not dead?!" Every single Tuesday night at practice, at some point, he would squeeze my arm, look me straight in the eyes, and ask, "How are you not dead?!" Every time, I would think, *That's a really long story, kid. Maybe when you're a little older?*

I was back to coaching all three of my boys' soccer and football teams. On Tuesday nights from 5:00 to 6:00 p.m., I coached Henry's team of five- and six-year-olds. From 6:00 to 7:00 p.m., I coached Walter's team of seven- and eight-year-olds. And from 7:00 to 8:00 p.m., I coached Asher's team of nine- and ten-year-olds. Every Saturday—game day—I spent all day on the football field. The commissioner was great about scheduling. I never had any overlaps or conflicts. It worked out flawlessly for me to coach every game.

Coaching three teams of eleven players each meant I was interacting with thirty-three kids every week—plus one or two parents per kid took that number up to seventy-five or eighty people. And do you know how many strange looks, comments, or awkward interactions I got from that group that season?

Zero.

Every one of my players and every parent seemed to be blind to my condition. To this day, I am really good friends with a lot of those families. Some of them ended up coming to our church, and I've been to their homes.

And my "How are you not dead?" little guy? Well, I have lunch with his dad every once in a while. We're all like family. My kids and I both built relationships with those families. Not only did no one ever bring up my lack of hands or legs, everyone was overly accommodating to me, trying to be helpful. They were all cautious about being in my way and made sure to pick up anything I dropped.

Asher became my assistant coach for Walter's and Henry's teams. Every Tuesday before practice, I would let him know what we were going to do, and he would be my hands and feet, showing the other kids how to do a drill or run a play. The kids and the parents loved him being involved. They called him Coach Asher. For Asher's team, my dad stepped in as my assistant coach, which was a lot of fun for both of us.

We had an incredible year. By the end of that first season, my boys' sports teams had become my catalyst for the confidence to get back to the things I have always loved about my life.

As the season was winding down, God threw me another curveball—this time, a really good one. In October 2020, Bart Millard called with a unique proposal from MercyMe.

Going Viral (in a Good Way)

"Hey Gary, you know that we've been working on our new album off and on for about two years," he said. "We wrote a song that's going on the record, and we were thinking about you. We want you to hear it. I'd like to send it to you and see what you think."

Wondering why the song might have some connection to me, I responded, "Sure, Bart, okay. I'll listen as soon as you send it to me."

I got the song. I listened. I wept like a baby and called Bart back before I had even stopped crying.

"We've all been watching your story unfold throughout this past year," he explained. "When we finished 'Say I Won't' and decided it would be a single, we knew we wanted to shoot a video. We saw on your latest Facebook post that you're getting your prosthetic arms soon. Would you allow us to tell your story through this song?"

Immediately, I teared up again. "I've been trying to figure out why all this has happened, and I know I have a story to tell," I responded. "If this can encourage people to follow Christ, no matter what they go through, then, yes, I absolutely want to do it."

On November 4, I went to a production facility in Nashville called the Steel Mill. We spent all day and late into the evening shooting the video for "Say I Won't" with Ryan Slaughter from TwoSevenTwo Productions—who had also been one of my roommates in Dallas when he and I worked for Shepherd Ministries. Ryan and his camera crew also came to our house to capture the moment on film when FedEx delivered my prosthetic arms. They spent all day getting various footage and interviews of our family. Those shots in the "Say I Won't" video of the first time I put my arms on are not a reenactment—they're the real deal. The shots of Mike and Robby in my hospital room were taken when MercyMe's tour got shut down during COVID and they both came to Florida to visit me.

In a behind-the-scenes video, Bart and the other guys shared, "We have stayed in touch with Gary over the years and been involved with multiple things with his family and his kids. That makes our opportunity to tell part of his story that much sweeter for us. We're just glad he trusts us enough to tell it. You're talking about somebody that has incurred some unbelievable hospital bills, so if there's any way we can do something to draw attention to his situation, to try to help him pay some of that, we just want to do everything we can to help, because he's been a part of our family for a long time. We're going to do our best with the video, but we're already proud of what we've been able to do with the song. We feel incredibly blessed and thankful for this opportunity and can't wait to see what comes of it."

To be clear, Bart didn't write the song about me or for me. But because the pandemic was making the album production take longer than usual, by the time of its release, they had decided to tweak some lines and connect me with the video. We all felt like my story gave the lyrics a unique context—the right context.

The video came together quickly, and on December 4, 2020, it debuted on YouTube. In January 2021, the single went to Christian radio. As of this writing, the "Say I Won't" video has 6.5 million views on YouTube.

As its popularity grew, the mainstream media began to pick up on the story. All our phones started ringing. I distinctly recall sitting in front of my refrigerator, still trying to figure out how to fill up a cup of water with ice by myself, when *Fox & Friends* called for an interview. I remember thinking, *What in the world is going on here?*

Then *Good Morning America* called, asking me and the band to do a Zoom interview with Will Reeve—son of the late actor Christopher Reeve—who's a reporter for ABC News. After the interview, Will and I stayed on the call and talked for another half hour. His father, who is best known for playing Superman, had been paralyzed in an equestrian event, and Will knew very well the things my kids and I were facing.

On the day my interview with Will was broadcast on *GMA3*, I was in Tampa at the International Institute of Orthotics and Prosthetics, a school where people go to learn to become prosthetists. In early 2021, I started going there occasionally to be a model for the students. For hours at a time, I sit on a table while they learn how to cast arms and legs. (Speaking of being a model, in October 2021, I was also one of twenty amputees chosen to walk the runway in a special fashion show in New York. I was so glad to be able to check "runway model" off my bucket list.)

At 1:00 p.m., we took a break from the students putting fiberglass all over my stumps for the molds so we could all watch the TV interview with me and MercyMe.

The guys in the band were accustomed to media interviews, but I still wasn't. Almost overnight, I was inundated with calls and messages. The volume was unbelievable. Only months before, I had been struggling with the fear of being in front of a soccer team full of six-year-olds and their parents . . . now I was on national TV. I experienced an odd mix of excitement and humility. One thing I came to know for sure: God most definitely has a sense of humor.

One of the most difficult parts of the sudden notoriety was literally being told hundreds of times a day how much of an inspiration I was or how motivational my story was. People were sending me pictures of themselves holding up cardboard signs that read "Say I Won't" like in the video. I also received lots of letters and cards from kids. All the while I was just trying to figure out my new life following my "fifteen minutes of fame."

One of the biggest blessings was that it took my long-standing friendship with the band to a new place. Because they were constantly being interviewed about my story, we were communicating all the time again. We still have a text thread called "MercyMe and the Amputee." We've always had a lot of fun together, and we still do.

After the video went viral, I received an email from a canine training company in Illinois, asking if I am a veteran. (I get that question quite often because of the nature of my amputations and the way I look.) I told them no, but they asked if I would be interested in having a service dog anyway; the owners had seen my story and wanted to provide me with a fully trained service dog at no charge.

Reading that email, I wept.

A week later, the company called to say they had acquired a sixth-generation, purebred, all-black, one-and-a-half-year-old German Shepherd on my behalf. He was medically cleared and fully trained.

When they asked what I wanted to name him, without any hesitation, I answered, "Ecmo!" I wanted to name my dog after the machine that saved my life. It made sense to me that if I screamed "Help!" he would become my "life support" by trying to get somebody's attention. He also had been trained to sniff out my cell phone, pick it up in his mouth, and bring it to me.

Also, if I say the word "brace," he will take a wider stance for me to lean on his 110-pound frame. That's really helpful when I'm putting on my prosthetics.

Ecmo became my 24/7 best friend. He knows when I don't feel well, when I'm sad, and when I'm happy. After Bones passed away during my hospitalization, there was no better gift for me than what Ecmo brings to my life every day.

But there was something else that happened during that season, too—a sad thing.

Different Paths

I'm sure you have probably wondered why I have referred to my spouse as my "wife-at-the-time." Here's the explanation.

After I was discharged from the hospital in May 2020, she was my primary caregiver and I, of course, was the patient. We were suddenly forced to take on new roles in our relationship. Although I worked hard to become as independent as I possibly could, for a while I was essentially helpless.

By January 2021, I had made some improvements and was able to do more on my own. Because we needed the money and she needed a break from caregiving, she went back to work in mid-March. Over the next few months, we began to grow distant from one another.

By August, we had a heart-to-heart conversation in which we honestly evaluated our marriage and mutually agreed to start the process of separation. The divorce was finalized on January 21, 2022.

While we each went our separate ways, she will always be the mother of our three amazing boys and the adopted mom of our incredible daughter. And for those God-ordained gifts, I will forever be grateful.

CHAPTER EIGHT

I'm Gonna Run. No, I'm Gonna Fly

In the spring of 2021, I celebrated one year of being out of the hospital as the media frenzy following the "Say I Won't" viral moment had started to calm down. That's when three of the pastors at my home church—the Church at Viera, or CAV—took me to lunch and asked if I would be willing to share some of my story in the upcoming Easter service.

The lead pastor, Mark Ragsdale, told me, "Gary, we've waited a year to talk to you about doing anything with us. After you got out of the hospital, we just wanted to be your church, for us to be your pastors. We know that since the release of the video, a lot of people have been coming after you. But now, we feel like it's the right time for us all to connect your story at the church. If you feel the same, we'd like to show the 'Say I Won't' video and then we'll do a five-minute interview."

I was both touched and impressed that they had waited for me to have some space from the trauma and then let the smoke clear from the viral moment. Waiting to give me an invitation like this meant a lot to me, and I was grateful to have such real and respectful people in my life.

Starting in 2020, our church began to hold the Easter service at a nearby USSSA baseball stadium, about a mile away from the main campus. More than six thousand people pack out the stands every year; I had never shared my story with that many people before. This would be very different from looking at an interviewer on a screen. On TV, there might be millions out there somewhere watching, but that never really computed to me. Being in front of thousands in real time would be my next step of faith. But I knew this was where God was leading me, so I agreed.

On that Easter Sunday morning, the church played the MercyMe video on the Jumbotron, and then I wheeled out to the pitcher's mound in my motorized chair to join the pastor. As planned, he interviewed me for about five minutes, asking me three questions: What happened, what are you doing now, and what's your goal for the future? Afterward, as the worship band started to play, I wheeled back off the field to go sit with my kids.

"Why Didn't He Walk Off?"

A lady named Stephanie, who had watched the service online that day, reached out to the pastor the following week and asked, "How come Gary didn't walk off the baseball field? It would have been incredible had he gotten up out of his wheelchair and walked off." The pastor, a bit surprised by her direct tone, politely answered, "Well, even though Gary has his prosthetic arms and legs now, he can't walk on them yet because it's still too painful."

"I work at POA, a prosthetics company in Orlando," Stephanie said. "Would you please reach out to Gary and ask him to contact us? We can help him."

I need to confess here that after Pastor Mark called to tell me about his conversation with Stephanie, I didn't contact POA right away. By that point, I had been to at least three prosthetic companies, and I was a bit weary *and* leery, because the outcome wasn't as simple as it had sounded. But I finally decided I had nothing to lose, so I got the number and reached out.

On June 5, 2021, I had my first appointment at POA and met Stan Patterson, the founder. Stan, who is a Godsend, looked at me and said, "You know, Gary, we're not breeding pandas here. This isn't that hard. I'm going to have you walking in two days and you'll be able to run a mile in thirty days."

I looked at him like he was crazy, and said, "It's been a year and you're the fourth prosthetic facility I've been to!"

Stan ignored my comment and just kept right on talking. "First, we're not going to size you, just pull something off the shelf, and have you put it on. We're going to cast your legs today and make everything custom to fit *you*."

And that's exactly what they did, immediately tackling the tedious process of casting me. On June 7, I went back to put on my new set of legs and not only stood up, but started walking. Yes, two days later—exactly as Stan had predicted—for the first time since I had gotten out of the hospital, I was walking again.

But even with that accomplishment, I still didn't believe that I could *run*. But Stan stood firm. "I'll have you ready to run a 5K within thirty days."

Because of all the attention I had gotten over the previous year, I now had a lot of people watching my story on social media. Because I had posted Stan's bold claim to everyone, I felt I had a responsibility to meet that expectation. So I started looking for 5Ks in my area.

I ended up finding a two-mile race set for August 15, almost two months away. Two miles in two months sounded much more reasonable to me under the circumstances than a whole 5K. So I signed up, announced my goal to the world, and was amazed by and grateful for the number of people who rallied around me.

Next, POA fitted me for running blades. Those are the big scoop-like prosthetics that you may have seen in the Paralympic Games. They are totally different than standard-style leg replacements, designed purely for shock absorption and speed.

Once the blades were done, I put them on and stepped onto an anti-gravity treadmill. I was practically floating as I learned how to run again.

The company that makes those specialty treadmills, AlterG Machines, reached out to me after seeing the video POA posted of me running. After hearing more of my story, they offered to sponsor me in the two-mile race. They also sent some folks to interview me while I was training on the AlterG machine.

On August 15, 2021, I finished my first race in 49 minutes and 22 seconds.

Around that time, I received an email from a pastor at a church called Cross Connection in Dodge City, Kansas, asking, "Hey, if we cover everything, would you come tell your story to our congregation?"

It turned out that a new believer named Darren Glenn had heard my story and asked if the church could bring me in to speak.

Having done the interview at my own church for Easter, I felt confident that I could tell another congregation what God had done in my life. I agreed and the date was booked—the first of many to come.

Faith Is Full of Surprises

On March 6, 2021, MercyMe invited me to join them on stage after they sang "Say I Won't" at a concert they were doing at the Ritz Carlton Hotel in Amelia Island, Florida. On cue, I wheeled out after the song. What I didn't know was that the guys had arranged a surprise for me.

When I reached center stage with Bart, the other guys wheeled out a new specialty wheelchair with crazy features like built-in speakers and USB ports. The chair could lift straight up eighteen inches. Now, if I'm talking to someone who is six-foot-five, I can raise the chair and look the person in the eye. The chair can flatten out to lie like a bed or stand me fully upright. The wheelchair company had even put a "Say I Won't" bumper sticker on the back.

As if that weren't enough of a blessing, that weekend I met two of my heroes. The first was John Lynch, the author of *The Cure*—the book Bart had taken me through to help me understand and begin to grasp God's grace. The second was Mark Stuart, former lead singer for the legendary Christian band Audio Adrenaline. Since high school, I have always loved their music.

A few hours before the concert, I had wheeled around the corner toward the lobby in my hotel to see Mark and John standing together! I fangirled right there in lobby.

As I wheeled up to them, John looked at me and said, "Gary Miracle!" I said exactly what I was thinking: "Oh my gosh, I can't believe you know my name!"

Both John and Mark graciously spent time talking with me. Afterward, John and I exchanged cell phone numbers. The next morning, I woke up to a text from him that said, "Hey, I don't know if you'll get this in time, but would love to meet you down in the lobby for coffee."

I texted back, "Absolutely." I could hardly get dressed fast enough! I was grateful for the chance to thank John for all the life-changing truth I had learned from his book.

After I had shared my full story with him, John said, "Gary, I'd love to step alongside you and be one of your mentors." Of course, I immediately agreed. I knew he would be an invaluable support to me as I was beginning to get regular speaking opportunities. At that time, he had just started a new endeavor called "John Lynch Speaks." That's how I also got the name of my ministry.

I officially started Gary Miracle Speaks in July 2021, and have had the privilege of speaking at a few events with John since then.

For my first speaking engagement in August 2021, Asher accompanied me to Dodge City, Kansas. From there, God chose to open the floodgates; it seemed like every morning I was waking up to another speaking invitation. But I knew these were not coming because of some marketing campaign or an agent making phone calls. No, God was bringing them. I was doing what He had intended for me to do. I was serving my new purpose in the new life He had ordained for me.

By that fall, I was speaking at churches, schools, and corporate events almost every weekend. As dark as so many of my seasons have been, I love that I am able to go out and bring light and hope to thousands of people by sharing my story.

For quite a while now, I have felt that God is driving the bus and I'm just along for the ride. He knows where we're going, so I just need to enjoy the journey. But that's actually the mission of the Christian life for any of us who call Him Lord! I didn't just decide to make a career change. I didn't just decide that God had called me to a new ministry and start finding churches where I could speak. He did it all—everything that He took away and all that He gave back. I was only responding to what He was bringing into my life.

As the invitations came in, I made the mistake of thinking I was supposed to say yes to every one. But I forgot a crucial truth: There's only one of me, and my kids only have one dad. When I began to miss my kids' games and other important events, I knew I was in trouble. I had to gain some wisdom quickly and make some hard adjustments to balance out my life and schedule.

In January 2022, I committed to keep speaking as long as God continued to open the doors, but I was going to be much more selective. To guide me in this balancing act, I asked John Lynch, Mark Stuart, and four other men to become my sounding board for any important decision regarding my family, ministry, or business. In asking God for His guidance and wisdom, I sensed He was leading me to create this group of men to stand with me. We have an ongoing group text; they all know they have an open invitation to speak into any decision I am making. I have given them full authority to say anything to me, and I will listen. Proverbs 11:14 tells us, "For lack of guidance a nation falls, but victory is won through many advisers" (NIV). The Message Bible states it this way, "Without good direction, people lose their way; the more wise counsel you follow, the better your chances." I have seen firsthand the amazing value of having counselors like those men in my corner.

Today, when someone asks me to speak at an event, I walk through a checklist to help me decide whether to say yes or no. If all the boxes get checked in the affirmative and I sense no red flags, I go. If there are some no's, I decline. (Sometimes, there are compromises, such as a changed date, etc.) I'm glad I only had a short season when things got too crazy. Getting back to all my kids' events and finding balance was a relief. Honestly, I know that most people are not going to remember the day Gary Miracle came to speak at their church, but my kids and I are going to remember the times I needed to be with them and wasn't.

Pushing Past the Darkness

In September 2021, the kids began spending only half of every week with me. I found that when they weren't at the house, I could quickly go to a very dark place. I had never had to live without them being around all the time—and when you're in a wheelchair, with so much you can't do for yourself, being alone is tough, physically, emotionally, and mentally.

That fear finally came to a head for me, ironically, on Halloween night—the first "holiday" my kids weren't with me. I was scared to drive my wheelchair around the house. I realized if something happened and I fell out, my only lifeline was Ecmo. As I mentioned in the previous chapter, if I call out "Help!" three times, he starts going crazy, barking. If nobody comes soon, he's trained to go find my phone and bring it to me. That was the only security I had living on my own, hoping that my dog would actually do what his trainers said he could do if something happened.

At around 5:30 in the evening, before I thought any neighborhood kids might come to the door, I went outside and unplugged all our inflatable decorations, then turned off all the lights in the house. I didn't want to see kids with their parents, smiling, laughing, and yelling, "Trick or treat!" and compare their togetherness with my loneliness.

My thoughts were overwhelming. The darkness was overpowering and overbearing. If there was ever a time I was going to harm myself, that would have been the night. I just wanted to fall asleep as quickly as possible. I had some sleeping medication the doctor had given me, so around 11:00 p.m., I took two pills that knocked me out quickly.

When I woke up the next morning, I had no idea what had happened or why the night before had been so much worse than any time I could recall. But my first thought was that everything was going to be okay. In fact, I woke up relieved, happy, and smiling. I got into my chair, turned on every light in the house, and cranked up MercyMe on my speakers. I was amazed how positive I felt—the polar opposite of the night before. For the next week or so, every day when I woke up, life seemed to get a bit easier. I was getting better and stronger. Healing and peace were alive in my heart. I was going to be okay.

The truth that Jesus lived, died, and rose again was giving me the ability to rise above all the stuff this world throws at me. And you can choose that truth, too. We can rise above all the things of our flesh and the accusations of the enemy. Jesus took care of it all, so we don't have to suffer from those things any longer.

I'm sharing this specific story with you because whatever you may have gone through in your life or are going through now, there is a way to get through the dark nights to the light of the morning. Those really dark times can feel like they will be the end of your life, but they don't have to be. You can make it. You can push through. You will get to the brighter days, but you have to press through the darkness to arrive where you need to be.

The positive changes in me must have been noticeable, because one day the kids said, "Dad, we've noticed you're not crying anymore." I smiled and told them, "Yeah, everything is starting to be okay." On Thanksgiving, looking around the table at my family, I realized that I was *more* than okay—I was truly thankful. I felt like my heart was beating again. I was starting to feel like me again.

One passage in the Bible that I often hold onto is Lamentations 3:22–23:

> The faithful love of the Lord never ends! His mercies never cease. Great is his faithfulness; his mercies begin afresh each morning.

There will never be a more amazing day than today. Yesterday is gone and tomorrow is always the *next* day. Today is all we have. And today, His mercies are new.

I felt those verses. I now put them on and wear them daily, and it is wonderful. And what is true for me is true for you, too.

Take that verse and make it your own, claim it as your own, just like I have.

CHAPTER NINE

Marriage Is a Ministry

Eventually, my kids ganged up on me concerning something I hadn't even thought about.

"Dad, put yourself back out there," Johana said. "You can do this. Go out on a date." When all four of your kids come into agreement on *anything* and present you with a united front, you'd better pay attention. I knew I couldn't dismiss them.

A few days later, I noticed a feature on Facebook: There was a tab that said "Dating" with a heart beside it. Curious, I clicked to read the description, decided to go for it, and set up a profile. I filled out all the generic info, like, "I'm Gary. I'm forty. I'm divorced. I have four kids." But then the next section said, "Add photos." I immediately thought of all the glamorized and filtered photos that people use on the internet, or the profile photos that are at least ten years old. I wasn't about to "catfish" anyone in my circumstances.

Any woman considering me needed to know the reality of my situation.

I started to think, *Okay, this is my moment. I've managed to be out on the soccer fields and that's gone much better than I expected. So if I'm going to "put myself out there," then I have to be true to who I am*. I uploaded my current full-body pictures, once again using the inspiration of *The Greatest Showman* song to say, "*This* is me." I hit the submit button with absolutely no idea what might happen.

Gary Miracle was now officially "back out there."

About a week after I submitted my profile, a local woman responded. We had a few harmless chats—superficial dialogue that lasted about a week. We never exchanged phone numbers or got together. *Well, if nothing else comes of this, at least someone responded and liked me back*, I thought. That made me feel really good and boosted my confidence. The woman obviously knew what I looked like. She had seen my picture and reached out anyway.

I took a break from the Facebook Dating page over the holiday. Christmas and New Year's would forevermore be connected to the horrible memories of when the nightmare began. I knew I had to push through and hope each year would get better.

In January 2022, I decided to get more serious about the dating idea, so I downloaded a dedicated app. I posted all the same info and pictures as before.

Through it, I soon met a great Christian woman in the area; we dated casually for about a month until we made a mutual decision not to move forward. Going from a chat to actual dating really helped me to be confident that I could have a real relationship. My kids were right.

Nonetheless, I had grown uncomfortable with online dating. Something just didn't feel right to me. So I deleted my profile. Instead, I committed my love life to the Lord, saying, "Okay, God, I'm leaving this completely up to You now. If You want me in a relationship, then You have to bring her to me in Your way and in Your time. And make it obvious . . . please."

A Stampede of Butterflies

Asher plays drums in the band at his school. Walter, Henry, and I went to his spring concert on a Friday. While we were sitting there, with me in the aisle in my wheelchair, I noticed a lady seated several rows in front of us. I had known *of* her for about five years. We had gone to the same church for a while and our kids had also been in the same homeschool group. But even with the interactions between our families, she and I didn't know each other.

I knew her name: Jenna Buzzo. She was now a resource teacher. My boys were in some of her classes and knew her three kids. They were all about the same age and attended the same school. I had heard she had gone through a divorce before I did, but her ex-husband was also at the concert, seated a few chairs down with their other children between them. I wondered if that meant they were working on getting back together.

As we sat there waiting for the concert to start, I couldn't figure out why she was so distracting to me. As crazy as this sounds and felt to me in the moment, I had that weird butterflies-in-the-stomach feeling. But it wasn't just a few flutters—more like a stampede. The emotion surprised me; it was like I couldn't help myself. I found myself repeatedly glancing her way, not thinking at all about the prayer I had prayed when I had turned my love life over to God.

For the duration of the concert, my attention was split between my son on the stage and the back of Jenna's head. I had no idea what was happening, but I liked it.

When the concert was over, the boys and I stayed where we were to allow the crowd to exit so as not to hold anyone up. Jenna had to go around me in my wheelchair, which caused us to make brief eye contact. We nodded politely and smiled at each other. There were the butterflies again—more warm, fuzzy feelings. But that was all that happened. One thing I knew: I didn't want to get in the way of any sort of reconciliation with her ex, so I would need to be careful with any attempt at communication.

Something about that evening had caused me to see Jenna in a new way. One of the unique but very real dynamics about being a divorced Christ-follower is that you have to come to accept when you are *allowed* to see someone of the opposite sex in a different way. I think that was a lot of what was happening: I knew I was being allowed to see Jenna in a new light, and that was okay.

That next week, the kids and I went on a spring break trip, but I couldn't seem to get Jenna off my mind. Not knowing what to do with the thoughts and feelings, I began to pray. I remember asking, "God, I don't know why I felt like I did when I saw her. I'm not sure why I saw her in that way. And I don't know why I'm *still* thinking about her. Please, help me figure this out."

On March 18, after the kids returned to school, I decided to reach out to Jenna through Facebook Messenger. But what should I say? I felt like I was back in high school, trying to figure out how to get the courage to ask the girl I knew was above my status to go to the prom.

So I skipped the high-school methods and went straight for a middle-school move: I sent a hand-wave emoji. That's it. No words. Not even "Hi." Just an emoji. (Yep, I know. Lame, right?)

I'm not sure if it was that day or the next, but Jenna sent back a much more committed message than I had offered: "Hi back." *Whoa, she actually used words*!

Okay, here's my shot. I have her attention. I messaged her back with something like, "Hey, I don't want to cross any lines here. I don't really know your situation with your ex, but could you just let me know?" She responded that she had been divorced for over a year and she and her ex-husband were simply working hard to coparent their three kids. That's why they were sitting on the same row at the concert.

So we started talking. Before long, our communication was every day, throughout the day. We were cautious not to let our kids know until we were both ready to share the relationship with them. It was important for us to protect all seven of them.

By the end of May, we were talking on FaceTime in the evening after the kids were all in bed. We would end up falling asleep with our screens still on. When my alarm would go off at 6:30 a.m., I would see her waking up too. We would then say goodbye to get our days started. We both made it clear early on that we didn't want to talk just to talk. Neither of us wanted to waste time or energy on something that wasn't serious; we weren't in the position to casually date. From the beginning, I knew I wasn't going to start bringing random women around my kids, and Jenna had committed to the same with guys. As a result, our conversations became increasingly honest, heartfelt, and intimate.

On one of our dates, Jenna told me her side of the story about the night of the concert.

"I knew you were sitting behind me, and I couldn't wait for the concert to end," she said. "I knew your story and I knew you were divorced. That's why, when I walked by you, I looked at you and smiled."

The dots were connected. That night, we both realized something was going on. I shared with her that next week after the concert, I had a feeling that we were going to be together somehow. I told her how I had prayed, finally gaining the confidence to reach out to her with my juvenile, yet very safe, hand-wave emoji.

The Blessed Blend

We eventually decided to break the news to our seven kids and let them in on the relationship. We agreed to meet at a local outdoor shopping mall that was a great gathering place for families. There was a huge fountain where my kids loved to run around and play where we could converge. But before I tell you about the family meeting, here's some important backstory.

At the Christian school where Jenna was a resource teacher, Asher and Walter would often go to her classroom to take their quizzes and tests. Both boys knew her as Ms. Buzzo. Jenna has two girls and a boy—Isabella, who was eleven at the time, Abigail, who was nine, and Joseph, who was seven years old.

When my three boys realized the lady I was dating was actually their resource teacher and who her kids were, and her kids realized who I was, everyone freaked out with excitement. The connection seemed to make sense to everybody, and life quickly began to fall into place. For the first couple of weeks, Asher kept coming up to me with a funny smirk on his face, giving me elbow high-fives, and saying, "Ms. Buzzo! Good job, Dad!"

One of the blessings was that six of our seven kids had an instant friend—someone their own age. However, Johana had a slightly longer adjustment period. Because she was the oldest and not connected the same way in school or by age, plus being very protective of her dad, she was understandably on the fence for a while. By that point, because she was eighteen, she had chosen to live with me full-time. From the day I had gotten home from the hospital, she had stepped up to help take care of me. So allowing another female to come into our lives took some time to navigate, which we all understood and accepted.

But, once again, God in His sovereignty had worked out every detail. At one point in her life, Jenna had run a group home for teenage foster girls in Fort Lauderdale and had personally fostered six daughters over the course of four years. So she was well prepared to deal with everything Johana was feeling, knowing what to do and what *not* to do. A lot of stepmoms and stepdads take any adjustment period or rejection personally, allowing it to create emotional wounds—but Jenna got it. She knew Johana needed grace and time. She would often reassure me, "Gary, I see her. It doesn't faze me. I know where she's at. I know what she's thinking. I've been trained in this. It's going to be okay."

When Jenna and I first began dating, I didn't make a list of all the qualities my perfect woman would have. But if I had done that, she would check every box on the list, even things I never knew I wanted. Because God is so good, He gave me "immeasurably more than all [I] could ask or imagine, according to His power that is at work within [me]" (Ephesians 3:20 NIV). When I thought back to how I had prayed, "God, if You want me to be with somebody, You're basically going to have to deliver that woman to me," I knew He had done just that.

I knew before proposing to Jenna that I had to reach out to my mentors for counsel. "If there's anybody who knows how fleeting and fast this life is, it's me," I said. "I don't want to waste any more time here." They all agreed that even though things with Jenna had happened fast, they could see that it was right.

On June 20, 2022, I bought the engagement ring that Jenna and I had previously chosen, then went home to start working on my proposal. We had already planned to go out to dinner that night, and I was determined to make everything perfect.

With some strategic help, I had everything prepared at the house for us to "swing by to pick something up" before heading to the restaurant. Flowers were laid out beside the ring, ready to go; my iPad was on the kitchen counter with a song cued up, ready to record the moment.

After picking Jenna up, I told her I had to run back by the house. While she was waiting in the car, I started the music, turned on the iPad to record, then texted her to come in for a minute. When she walked in the door, I was down on one knee, ready.

Everything went off without a hitch, and Jenna said yes. And there was video captured to prove it! I had arranged for our families to meet us at the restaurant afterward to celebrate, and we had a super-fun evening.

But as it turned out, the celebration was just getting started.

The next day was my grandmother Gigi's eighty-ninth birthday. She is the godliest woman I've ever known, a rock of faith. I called to wish her a happy birthday and share my good news. While we were on the phone, another call came in: My grandfather, Gigi's ex-husband, had passed away earlier that morning.

With all kinds of emotions going on, I called Jenna to tell her what happened. "When we get married, I want Gigi to be there," I said. "I want her to meet you and I want her to experience what is happening in my life. Because now, it's too late for my grandpa, he can't."

As our conversation went deeper, we arrived at the same question: "What if we just go get married? . . . With no one there? Why *are* we waiting? Why *should* we wait?"

We couldn't find a reason. I called my parents and Jenna called her mom. They were all excited for us. We decided that at one o'clock we would go to the courthouse and get married. (If you're tracking the time, yes, this was only about twelve hours after we had gotten engaged.) My assistant, Tracy, and Johana came with us to be our two witnesses.

It was June 21, 2022—almost four months after that first butterfly stampede.

When the Real Work Begins

That's the Hallmark Channel version of our story. But as many married couples find, there was another side of the coin I want to share a part of our lives, particularly for those who are navigating new relationships, that I could have easily left out.

During our first month together, things got really dark for us both. Neither of us had any idea how marriage would be a trigger on every front—emotionally, mentally, physically, and spiritually. We were both still healing from our previous wounds but felt like we were each in a really healthy place. When you truly commit in a marriage and start life together 24/7, a strange mirror gets held up to your face and you see yourself through someone else's eyes. That process reveals there's a *lot* more to work through than you previously thought.

The initial challenge took place on our honeymoon. We had booked Jenna's dream trip to New York City. The morning after our wedding, when we were supposed to head to the Big Apple, we woke up to a message that our flight was delayed, which then turned into a cancellation. That glitch started a chain reaction that resulted in our entire trip being called off. Right out of the gate, I felt like a failure as a new husband. The fiasco *had* to be all my fault. Jenna was understandably disappointed about how things were playing out in our first days as newlyweds.

I was already scheduled to be in Nashville on June 24 for a NASCAR race that I was involved with as a sponsor. Jenna and I ended up having to stay a second night at the airport hotel. So, we just decided to go on my business trip together, leaving for Nashville a day early. The bottom line is, we had an awful first week. Once the triggers started, the miscommunications began, which complicated matters and caused our walls to go up.

Emotional and intellectual intimacy are just as key for a successful marriage as physical intimacy. But if you've been through a divorce, many of those aspects are either held back, buried deep, or neutralized during the season of being single again. When a new union with a different person is introduced, old wounds can quickly resurface.

Jenna and I were struggling to the point of questioning if we had made a mistake, so we talked it over with our pastor. He listened intently, and then said, "I think neither of you realized what it would feel like to be married again. But clearly, you're both still carrying past hurts with you that you'll have to somehow let go of to move forward.

"The good news is I actually think there's a lot of hope here. So I want to ask that, for the next thirty days, you agree to hit the reset button. Promise that you're going to give each other *everything* you've got in this marriage. Don't hold *anything* back. Give each other grace and the benefit of the doubt. You have a wide-open canvas here to rewrite your stories and decide what *this* marriage is going to look like."

Together, we committed to do exactly that. We knew we loved each other and wanted our relationship to work, so we had to push past all the roadblocks and lingering issues. We started over with a blank slate, expecting the best of one another. We let our guards down. Very soon, Jenna allowed me to lead her, and I was allowing her to support me. I was letting her be a stepmom to my kids, and she was letting me be a stepdad to hers. We did our best to live out the marital truth of Ephesians 5:21: "Submit to one another out of reverence to Christ."

As we applied all these dynamics to our marriage over the next few weeks, fulfillment settled in as we gave each other the space, grace, and freedom to excel in our roles as spouses and parents. The hard work paid off in those thirty days, just as our pastor had expected. One of the changes that really helped us as a couple was to refer to our marriage as our ministry: Our two-becomes-one union is a ministry *to* each other and *with* each other as we serve God daily.

Over the next few months, we settled in and found our groove as husband and wife. Fast-forward to October 9, 2022. That's when we decided it was time to celebrate with an official wedding reception, inviting family and friends to one of our favorite local restaurants. As the evening was winding down, my best friend, Joe—the one who'd watched the Super Bowl with me in the hospital—put his arm around my shoulders, and said, "Hey, Gary, I need to tell you something that I've not shared with you yet." Seeing how serious he was, I tuned in.

"Every Sunday when I pulled into the hospital parking lot to go in and spend the day with you, I sat there and prepared myself for what I was going to say if you asked me to pull the plug or smother you with a pillow," he continued. "What would I do if you asked me to help you end your life? I just saw how horrible things were for you. I saw the pain and the questions. The days we cried together, wondering how this could have happened to you. So I got myself ready in case you ever asked me to help you take yourself out."

Joe paused, got teary-eyed, then said with a huge smile, "But, man, Gary, look at you now! You're married to a great woman. Your kids are doing so well. God has given you a plan and a purpose for your life in a way you would never have dreamed could happen." He punched me in the chest, like he always does, and then gave me a huge bear hug.

Those are the moments that make you stop and savor life, the ones you have to rest in—moments you are grateful to experience. When you feel like life has dealt you such a severe blow that you can't possibly see how to recover, you have to find a way to keep hope alive. And maybe someday, the best friend who walked through Hell with you will remind you that God is still good, and you are still alive to tell the world about it.

CHAPTER TEN

Living the No-More-Bad-Days Life

That's it. There's my story.

So here, in this final chapter, I'd like to flip the script. You've heard all about me. Now, I want to talk to you. Anywhere I speak, I tell my story and then turn the focus to the people in the seats because one thing is for sure: We all have struggles. Because of that, we all need hope. We all need help.

As humans, we deal with the same pervasive issues, like fear, insecurities, and doubts. Then there are specific battles like addictions or abuse; sometimes they stem from things others have done to us, sometimes from things we've done to ourselves. Each of us has battles we constantly fight within our hearts and minds. Some are on the front burner, while others simmer in the back.

Regardless of what your struggle may be or how it came about, my goal is to offer you some practical steps for living out a No More Bad Days lifestyle.

Maybe you're thinking, *No, Gary, actually right now, I'm good. Everything is great.* Well, that's awesome, but I still recommend you buckle up with the rest of us, because life can change all too quickly. I'm not trying to be negative, just realistic; remember that I was fine on Christmas Day, thought I was coming down with the flu on December 26, and by January 1, I had coded in the ER.

Most likely, the main difference between me and you is that my struggles are visible. If you were in my home, you could see how difficult it is for me to hold my toothbrush. You could see how hard it is for me to reach into a cabinet, grab a cup, go to the refrigerator, and fill it up with ice and water. You could physically see all my daily struggles. But there's a good chance that most of your struggles are *not* visible.

I know from all the years I lived before I lost my limbs that the invisible struggles can eat us alive, slowly consuming us from the inside out without anyone else ever knowing. No one can physically see anxiety, depression, insecurity, or self-hatred, but that doesn't make them any less real or destructive. Although the expressions and effects of those struggles are sometimes visible, most often, they are pushed down deep and hidden from sight.

Then there are external challenges, like finances and paying the bills. Right now, a lot of people are wondering where their next meal will come from. Some are in debt up to their eyeballs with no idea how to crawl out of the hole they have dug for themselves.

How about you? You can fill in the blank with your own battles. What is eating you alive that is invisible to everyone around you? What struggle do you dare not share with anyone? Where are you afraid to show your weakness? How hard are you trying to make sure no one can tell you don't have it all together?

As sinners, none of us want people to know who we really are underneath our masks. The thought of being vulnerable scares us to death. I know, because it took me thirty-nine years to be able to get to a place where I was *forced* to show my struggles. My physical battles suddenly made all my invisible issues *very* visible. For years, I tried to pretend everything was okay and I had it all together. I was good at hiding, which helped me put on whatever persona I felt the situation called for—the funny guy, the athlete, the musician, the good Christian, the life of the party. I couldn't let anyone know who I really was underneath my mask.

I've learned that our struggles find their power when they stay hidden. But as I took up the challenge to share mine, both visible and invisible, I found people actually responded in the opposite way than I had feared. I found out I can be loved despite my struggles. I am not judged because of them. I found that as I began to open up and share my pain, instead of people turning their backs on me or rolling their eyes and walking away, many responded with a resounding, "Me too! I'm struggling, too. I just didn't know how to say it. I wasn't brave enough to let anyone in."

Today, I, Gary Miracle, am living proof that sharing your struggles can create a village of people who pour into you, stand with you, stay with you, and allow you to do the same with them. With my huge list of visible struggles, I have had to receive help and grace. That acceptance has led to finding support with my invisible struggles as well. Then I realized the value of offering that same ministry and grace to others. I found that you can take all the energy you expended hiding and invest it in helping.

Now, let's look at some practical ways we can apply the truths found in a No More Bad Days life.

The Fork

If you and I were having dinner together, you would quickly see how difficult it is for me to hold onto my fork. There's a really good chance that, at some point in the meal, maybe more than once, I will drop that fork. When that happens, I know beyond a shadow of a doubt that you would reach down, pick up my fork, and hand it back to me. I wouldn't have to ask, and I bet you wouldn't even think about it. Your instinct would be to immediately help me, probably to keep me from feeling any embarrassment. I bet you would step in to serve me with joy in your heart and a smile on your face.

I'll venture to say there are more people in your life who would reach down to pick up *your* "fork" than you could possibly imagine.

The big questions are:

Who knows what your fork is?

How are you struggling to hold onto it right now?

What have you already dropped?

What are you going to do if you have no idea how to reach down and pick it back up?

How long are you going to stare at it lying on the floor before you let someone help you?

As you read those questions, your "fork" came to mind—your struggle. Your pain. Maybe more than one thing comes to mind.

Maybe you think no one else knows about your fork. But Someone does know. His name is Jesus.

Many scriptures talk about the benefits and blessings of helping each other pick up our forks when we discover we're part of a proactive community in Christ. Here are a few:

> "For where two or three gather together as my followers, I am there among them." (Matthew 18:20)

> As iron sharpens iron, so a friend sharpens a friend. (Proverbs 27:17)

> Confess your sins to each other and pray for each other so that you may be healed. (James 5:16)

> Share each other's burdens, and in this way obey the law of Christ. (Galatians 6:2)

> Don't look out only for your own interests, but take an interest in others, too. (Philippians 2:4)

> So encourage each other and build each other up, just as you are already doing. (1 Thessalonians 5:11)

> "So now I am giving you a new commandment: Love each other. Just as I have loved you, you should love each other. Your love for one another will prove to the world that you are my disciples." (John 13:34–35)

The Village

God the Creator designed us to live life with other people in a community. That's what I call "my village." Those are the people who didn't turn their backs on me when life got hard, when it was messy and time-consuming and uncomfortable. People in my village saw me drop my fork, picked it up, handed it to me, and just kept on doing that as time went by. No matter how many times I drop it, my village is there—and I do everything I can to pick up their forks, too.

My village isn't big, but the love the people in it have for me is deeper than I ever imagined. Feeling loved enough to be vulnerable with my visible struggles is what gave me the courage to open up and share all my *invisible* struggles, too. I'm not talking about shouting them from the rooftops or oversharing on social media. There are a lot of people out there who can't handle your struggles and burdens, and don't want to. They won't bear them in the way you need. But there will likely be at least two or three people in your life who will show up even at crazy hours when you call for help.

Whether you realize it or not, *you* have a village too. And whether you will admit it or not, you *need* your village.

No matter how difficult it may be, you need someone you can call and say, "This is the real me. This is who I am. I'm struggling with (blank), and I don't want anybody to know about all this ugliness." The right person will respond with something like, "Thank you so much for being honest with me. Let me link arms with you and let's do life together."

Jesus told us in John 10:10, " The thief comes only to steal and kill and destroy" (NIV). The thief—God's enemy, Satan—will tell us that no one is there for us, no one cares, and we're a fool to think otherwise. That's exactly why we can't listen to him. Jesus showed us the alternative He offers: "I have come that they may have life, and have it to the full. I am the good shepherd. The good shepherd lays down his life for the sheep" (NIV). Most often, the thief is going to come for us in the dark of night, when we're most vulnerable. He'll take anything he can possibly get his hands on. His only goal is our destruction. But while we must be alert, we can't fixate on him coming to attack us. We must keep our eyes on the Good Shepherd.

When you go through horrible circumstances in life, when things get dark and you experience loss and failure, you must remember that is not who you are. What you are going through at any given time doesn't define you. Instead, choose to say, from this moment on, "I will stand up and pledge 'No more bad days!'" If you can take that stance and look to Christ in every situation, not allowing the thief to gain a foothold, then you can find life at its fullest.

In Jeremiah 29:13, God tells us, "You will seek me and find me when you seek me with all your heart" (NIV). When we seek Him, it's almost unbelievable how He will manifest His presence in our lives. We can be intentional in a No More Bad Days attitude when we see all of life—the good, the bad, and the ugly—as an opportunity. We can see His grace in all things.

Like the herd of sheep protected by the shepherd, life is best found inside a village of people with like hearts and minds who are seeking Christ together.

The ID

Another well-known scripture that has come to mean a great deal to me as a powerful and personal truth is Galatians 2:20:

> My old self has been crucified with Christ. It is no longer I who live, but Christ lives in me.

No matter the circumstances or how bad the day may be, through Christ I have both the ability and the opportunity to say,

"It is no longer Gary who lives, but Christ lives in Gary." When people tell me, "You're such an inspiration," or "I don't know that I could have walked through that as well as you have," my response every time is, "It's not Gary Miracle who's doing this, but Christ in Gary. What you see in me and on me is His strength, courage, and, ultimately, His grace that reigns when I seek Him with all my heart."

What I say to those people, I now want to express to you: There's nothing you can't overcome with His strength, either.

Read or write your name in the blanks:

"It is no longer __________ who lives, but Christ lives in __________."

When we seek Him, we will find Him. When we find Him, we can live in Him. With humans, we're always playing hide-and-seek. With God, it is always seek-and-find. That's His promise, not mine. When we look for Christ in every circumstance, we will find His grace.

Now, this will always be easier said than done. It's not as simple as a Sunday school answer, because there will be days when we honestly confess, "I don't want to seek God right now. I don't want to believe that He is good, because this hurts way too much. What I'm going through makes me feel like everything He has ever given me is just being taken away. I feel like He's ripping something from me. It's easier for me to feel sad. It's easier for me to feel hurt than to feel hopeful." Have you ever felt like that? The truth is that we all have, and we all do. That's why understanding the truth of "Christ in me" is so vital to our journey.

With the thousands of people I have met in my life, I've never met one who said, "I really wish I hadn't chosen to live for Christ.

It's been such a horrible decision." But I do hear the polar opposite. People who have chosen to daily trust Him with their lives are always grateful they did. Because in and through Him, the opportunity is there to look at pain, loss, and even death very differently than before we knew Him—differently than the way the world sees them. This is why I take every opportunity to plead with people, "Please learn from my mistakes. Please learn from my journey. Please learn from what I have gone through. Choose Jesus and never look back."

Earlier in this book, I mentioned how I felt a connection to Job through my struggles that I never would have understood without them. No, I didn't lose as much as he did, but I can certainly relate to his journey. I understand his questions. How did the devastation in his life fit into God's plan? For me, the biggest truth of his story is found after all the dialogue with his "friends" and the monologue from God, when Job arrives at a life-changing conclusion:

> Then Job replied to the LORD:
> "I know that you can do anything, and no one can stop you. You asked, 'Who is this that questions my wisdom with such ignorance?' It is I—and I was talking about things I knew nothing about, things far too wonderful for me. You said, 'Listen and I will speak! I have some questions for you, and you must answer them.' I had only heard about you before, but now I have seen you with my own eyes." (Job 42:1–5)

I have been a Christian since I was a child. I played drums on the worship team in the youth band. I was a youth pastor on a church staff. I traveled with a Christian band, listening to them singing about Jesus and sharing the Gospel every night. I went to ministry school. But before my illness, I realized I had only heard *about* God. After dying, coming back, losing my limbs, and my first marriage ending, now I know what it means to have seen Him with my own eyes.

Does it have to take a crisis or a tragedy for us to get to that place of brokenness and humility? Maybe not. But the truth is, we aren't going to volunteer to be broken. We must be brought to that place by circumstances that God allows for our best.

Every time we interact with a fellow Christ-follower, we get to see Jesus in that person with our very own eyes. Looking back, I missed that important fact for far too long. But now I'm able to see it and, in fact, I look for it. I seek Him and find Him for myself, but I also seek Him and find Him in the lives of the people in my village.

I believe I serve a God who not only doesn't make mistakes, but cannot make mistakes. Because that's what perfection means. He didn't make a mistake in what happened to me. He didn't mess up my life—and He hasn't messed up with you, either. He has placed you in this very moment, at this very time, reading these words while going through your own circumstances—all this to give you exactly what He has for you in His perfect timing. As Christ-followers, we have to realize that what we go through is about having our life fall into place as God transforms us into the image of Jesus.

So many of us have been taught that the harder we work, the more we get. When we become adults, we are told that the more time we invest in our job, the more promotions we can get and the more money we can make. Spiritually, we are taught the same concept: The more good and the less bad we do, the better person we become. But when we're feeling distant from the Lord or that something is missing, we tend to look at our lives and say, "Well, I must not be praying enough. I'm not reading my Bible enough. I'm not going to church enough. I'm not being generous enough." Spiritually and emotionally, we beat ourselves up, thinking we're not *doing* enough.

When I walked through my transformation in grace, I realized there's no verse in the Bible to support the "not doing enough for God" mindset. It's no longer about what we do; it's about what Christ has done. If Christ is alive in us, then life is about who we are, not what we *do*. Now, when I feel like life is hitting the fan and I'm having the worst day possible, I can say it's Christ in me that can overcome anything. Not me—Christ *in* me. That is my ID—my new identity in Him.

A few months after Jenna and I got married, I changed her name in the contacts list on my cell phone from Jenna to "Christ in Jenna" because I want to see Christ in my wife. The next time I was driving down the road by myself and a text from her popped up on my dash screen, I had Siri read it to me. At the end of the message, it asked if I wanted to respond. When I said yes, the electronic voice asked, "What would you like to say to Christ in Jenna?" It surprised and amazed me to hear Jenna's name read back exactly as I had put it into my contacts list.

She was reading a Christian book and had shared an insight with me. Whatever "profound truth" I normally would have responded with quickly left me. In that moment, all I wanted was to express gratitude and encouragement to her.

Now, every time the electronic voice asks me what I want to say to my wife, hearing her name in that context changes how I speak to her and what I say. I'm no longer talking to Jenna, but Christ in Jenna. This makes me want to be gentler. To be a safe place for her. To be someone she can come to with both good things and hard things. I don't want to just respond or react, but receive and look for Christ in anything we're going through. That attitude changes everything about my identity and how I see others.

The Repeat

I believe I serve a Do-It-Again God. On the first day, He made the sun to shine. Then He looked at it and said, "Whoa, that is beautiful! Tomorrow, I'm going to do it again. I'm going to create more." So He did. When He created a flower, He looked at it and said, "Oh My goodness, look at that! So beautiful. I want to do it again, millions more times."

When my boys were little and we were playing in the backyard, I would grab them and throw them into the air as high as I could. Anyone watching often said, "Gary! That looks so dangerous. Be careful." I'll admit there were times I threw them a little higher than I should have. But every time, when they landed safely in my arms, they would look at me with a massive grin and say, "Do it again, Dad! Do it again!"

I have this vision of Christ looking at me after I have gotten honest with someone about my life and saying, "Wow, great job. I'm so proud of you for being vulnerable enough to call your friend and tell him that. For sharing what no one else knew when you were concerned you might be judged. Do it again!"

I thank God that I have people in my life with whom I can share my deepest secrets, my hurts, and my sins. I thank God that I can return the grace and be a safe place for those friends. People I can call and say, "I have to tell you what I just saw." Or the thought I just had. Or what I just said about someone under my breath. I believe that when we actually carry out James 5:16: "Confess your sins to each other and pray for each other so that you may be healed," Christ says, "Wow, that is amazing. I'm so proud of you for being vulnerable and courageous and brave enough to share your heart." As the Do-It-Again God, He then adds, "Please do it again tomorrow. Be the most real, the most authentic disciple of Mine that you can possibly be. Don't put on the mask to hide who you really are."

I know that decision is not easy. It's way easier said than done. I know how difficult it is to swallow your pride and confess your sin and pain. But, just as I had to learn, when you choose to get that invisible struggle outside into the light, you will find out that you are loved and not judged.

I still use a situation that happened when I was in high school to check myself. One Friday night after a football game, I was at a party, like always. I was holding court with my red solo cup, acting like I was drinking a beer. I was working hard to look good, be cool, and be accepted.

Out of nowhere, a guy came up to me and said, "I'm never going to become a Christian, because I see what you're doing right now, but I also see you on Wednesday nights at the youth group. You're such a hypocrite. You're all hypocrites."

I was speechless. I knew I was busted—guilty as charged. And I suddenly realized how my life and choices might affect someone else for eternity. That punch-in-the-gut moment has stayed with me like it happened yesterday.

I know that is not a cross I need to carry any longer. I know the Holy Spirit is bigger than that moment, and He could reach that guy a thousand different ways to overcome my poor witness. I believe in that moment, God was disciplining me to rethink my choices. I was called out for pretending to be somebody I wasn't. I was telling myself the Friday-night version of me was the pretender and the Wednesday-night guy was the real me. But who else was going to give me the benefit of the doubt like that? If one kid had the guts to say that to my face, how many other kids saw me but didn't speak up? I may have affected them in the same way.

In that moment, I felt worthless. I felt that I had no value and nothing to offer anyone. I felt that nobody would ever want to follow me, whether I was a Christian or not. That's the problem with being double-minded that James 1:8 and 4:8 tell us about: guilt and shame can rule you.

I wish I could say I never went to another Friday night party. I wish I could say I never held another red solo cup again. But I can't. It was quite a while before I stopped living that chameleon life.

In those moments when we know we have hurt someone, I believe God is saying, "Please don't do that again. Go back to what I do with you and in you." In those convicting moments, the point is not to beat ourselves up for what we've done or said; it's to learn from the mistake, repent, and move on. Remember, His specialty is grace and mercy that gives again and again and again.

The Invitation

If you have realized in reading these pages that you don't have a relationship with Jesus, let me share with you how to begin.

Romans 10:9–10 (ESV) states,

> If you confess with your mouth that Jesus is Lord and believe in your heart that God raised him from the dead, you will be saved. For with the heart one believes and is justified, and with the mouth one confesses and is saved.

If you decide to invite Him into your life by faith, you will receive His gift of forgiveness, grace, and mercy. Below is a prayer, should you need one as a guide. But the important thing is to share your heart with Jesus. Talk to Him as you would a best friend. Be as honest and specific as you can about what you need Him to do in your life.

Dear God, I know I am a sinner and need Your forgiveness. I now turn from my sins and ask You into my life to be my Savior and Lord. I choose to follow You, Jesus. Thank You for dying for me, saving me, and changing my life. In Jesus's name, amen.

If you prayed that prayer for the first time, congratulations: Today is your day of salvation, the day you met grace. A great next step would be to let someone know. It's time to build your village. Reach out to someone who is a Christ-follower. If you don't know any, go to the page titled "So, Where Can I Go from Here?" and scan the QR code. Reach out to us at Gary Miracle Speaks and let us know you prayed the prayer from this book to invite Christ to be your Lord. We want to celebrate with you.

If you are already a Christ-follower but realize you have been wearing a mask for far too long, beating yourself up about what you've said or done—simply apologize, and repent right away. Remember that on the day you met grace, Christ didn't hold anything back from you. He gave you everything He's got. You have His full power and authority inside you right now to repent—stop, turn around, and run to Jesus. Maybe you are someone who is not ready to ask Christ into your life. Or maybe you are already a Christian who is walking with the Lord. Either way, as you finish this book, I encourage you to go for a walk alone and talk to Him.

Talk to Him about your fork—whatever you're struggling to hold onto, whatever you keep dropping, however you need help to start or stop something.

Talk to Him about your village—the people you need to invite into your life on a deep level. Ask Him to help you find at least one person you will have the courage to contact and say, "Listen, I have to tell you something about me." Find someone you can trust to share whatever is on your heart.

Talk to Him about your ID and how you desire to live out "Christ in you," as well as see Him in others.

Talk to Him about what you need Him to do again for you—or anything you know you need to never do again.

Invite Jesus Christ into every aspect of your life. Keep Him the center of your attention.

I believe you'll find, just as I have, that by sharing your struggles, any stronghold in your life can be broken. You'll be able to move forward. You can be freed from whatever may be keeping you stuck. The enemy will never stop whispering in your ear to remind you of every bad thing you have ever said or done, so push past his accusations and look to the Shepherd—Jesus.

Those things we don't want anyone else to see or know or hear about can and will start chipping away at our hearts. The broken pieces can begin to pile up. When we make a bad decision, the temptation is to think, *Oh well, I guess this is me. I'm stuck here again. I guess this is my lot in life.* When Satan tries to grab you by the ankles to stop you from taking another step, that's when we follow the counsel of James 4:7: "So humble yourselves before God. Resist the devil, and he will flee from you." God can give us both a strong offense and a strong defense. The offense is humbling ourselves before God and the defense is resisting the devil. The result is a win: the enemy "will flee from you."

I want to encourage you to just love Jesus. The Bible tells you over and over again that He is madly in love with you. When the bad days show up, let your new mindset allow you to declare, "Not today, Satan." Your words and actions don't and won't define you. They are *not* who you are.

As my dear friend John Lynch writes in *The Cure*, "I am no longer a saved sinner. I am a saint who sometimes still sins." That is who you are because of Christ in you. That is your identity.

No More Bad Days is not a mantra, a religious concept, or a denial of reality. It is the Christ-empowered, God-given ability to choose life, as well as "love, joy, peace, patience, kindness, goodness, faithfulness, gentleness, and self-control" (Galatians 5:22–23).

The Apostle Paul tells us about a mindset Christ offers us. I want to repeat a very powerful command he gave us that you saw at the beginning of this book:

> We destroy arguments and every lofty opinion raised against the knowledge of God, and take every thought captive to obey Christ. (2 Corinthians 10:5 ESV)

Even though you will always have struggles and tough circumstances, you have the opportunity to take every thought captive in Christ. Through Him alone, you can choose to believe that your circumstances do not define you. Starting right now, my friend, by surrendering everything in you to Jesus, you can begin the journey of the No More Bad Days life.

Acknowledgments

Mom: you were there for me both times I came into this world. Thank you for always smiling ten miles wide, for being the prayer warrior, and for being one of the most godly, loyal women I know who has fought for me all my life.

Dad: for being one of my best friends on the planet and allowing Christ to transform who you are instead of transferring who you used to be before Him. It will be a giant win if I can be half the dad that you are to me.

Jennifer: for constantly loving and encouraging me and calling me your hero even though I feel like you've taught me most of what I know. Having the greatest sister ever has taught me how to be a brother.

Daryl: for always dropping whatever you're doing to come help me with whatever I need, like fixing something at my house, being my barber, and always making yourself available and reminding me that you're always there to talk if I need it.

My nephews: Joey—for trusting me enough to allow me into every area of your life. Being your uncle is a gift. Michael—for feeding me my baked ziti every Friday night in the hospital and for teaching Henry what it looks like to be a Christian.

My kids: Johana—for choosing to stand with me through it all and being my hands and feet when nobody else was there. One of the greatest privileges of my has been to call you my daughter and you allowing me to be your dad! Asher—my mini-me, for never leaving my side when we are together. You are always looking for anything I may need and stepping into it. I pray that you never lose your desire to become a doctor who helps people like my doctors helped me! Walter—for simply being Walter. For turning a blind eye to everything I was going through and never treating me any differently and always staying true to who you are no matter what I was going through or what that looked like. Henry—for running toward me every time I call your name, even if I just have a question you could've answered from afar. When you hear me say your name, you run to me—just in case. I love you all so much. I'm so thankful I'm still here to be your dad. I also pray that none of you lose your sense of humor about who I am and how I look. You all make me want to be better.

Jenna: for saying "hi" back. Christ's timing is everything. You matter so much to me. I know through and through that I am a better man, father, and husband because of the value you bring to me. I never want to go back to the days before you. You level me!

Tina Zimmerman: for reaching out and giving me a gift I didn't think was possible in ECMO, my service dog.

Tracy LaMonica—the first employee of Gary Miracle Speaks: for being so selfless and putting my needs and my family's above your own.

Robert Noland: you are more than a ghostwriter, more than an author, more than someone who helped me package words into a book. You're a friend, a safe place, and someone who fiercely protects me.

Dave Schroeder: for always being steady, guiding me, and having the gentlest voice—even when you might be having a bad day—to love on me and point me in the right direction. And for always reminding me that my identity and my heart come before a book.

Joe Mollica: for sitting in my hospital room for ten hours every Sunday. Whether in complete silence, crying, or talking and laughing, you were always there and you still are. You are my best friend!

Mark Ragsdale: My leader. My shepherd. My friend. My mentor. My sushi buddy. And my pastor! The gift you are to me is difficult to put into words. You are easy to follow because I know you are following Him. I can't wait for a lifetime of ministry alongside you.

MercyMe—Bart, Mike, Barry, Nate, and Robbie: Our friendship over the last twenty-plus years is something for which I will forever be grateful. The gift you gave me in telling my story in the "Say I Won't" music video has been nothing short of life-changing. Every one of you are family to me.

Scott Brickell: for being the bluntest, most brutally honest man I know, who will yell at me, ignore me, give me advice, lead me, and pray with me all at the same time.

John Lynch: for allowing Christ to live in and speak through you in a way that calms my heart every time we speak. You are so gentle. You are so loving. You are so safe. You will always be one of my heroes.

Mark Stuart: for going from someone I grew up idolizing as the best front man in the Christian music industry to someone I had the opportunity to meet, to someone I had the opportunity to get to know, to someone I now can't imagine my life without. You're constantly diving in (even when I don't want you to), asking me the tough questions, and pulling out the difficult answers.

If I forgot your name, I'm deeply sorry. For every person who never left my side and for every person who has joined my village since my life changed, I will forever be grateful. For those who decided to take another path, I'm sorry if it's my fault, and I ask for forgiveness. If that's not the case, please know that I'm grateful for the purpose you served in my life, and I'm thankful for the time that you were part of it.

Where Can I Go from Here?

If, for any reason, you can't find someone to be honest with about your life, you can reach out to us at Gary Miracle Speaks. Scan this QR code with your phone to go to my website. Click on the No More Bad Days tab in the header; that will take you to our Contact Form. I assure you we will respond and use our resources to help point you in the right direction.

Miracle's Miracles

- The family member knowing about the ECMO machine and hearing from God to make that recommendation
- A hospital that had an ECMO machine being forty-five minutes away
- The helicopter delay causing me to arrive at Advent in Orlando at the best possible time
- The ER staff not cutting off or removing my oxygen after coding
- The ER nurse checking my pulse one more time
- Dr. Bogar sensing that she needed to stay around the hospital after her shift had ended at 7:00 a.m.
- My family seeing the machine change from 40 to 100 after praying
- My dog Bones somehow appearing in my hospital room to tell me goodbye
- The plastic surgeon being approved for all four of my amputations
- The infectious disease doctor choosing the one right antibiotic out of twelve possibilities
- Being able to keep all my joints to receive prosthetics

- Stephanie from POA watching our church's Easter service and then contacting my pastor to offer their prosthetic services so I could walk and run again
- Jenna choosing me
- My friendship with MercyMe

APPENDIX

Witnessing a Miracle

I asked Dr. Linda Bogar, my dad, and my best friend to share their perspectives on my journey that began December 26, 2019. I also wanted you to hear from Jenna. If someone you love ever goes through a tragedy like mine, I hope that their selfless and sacrificial contributions will encourage and inspire you to follow their examples.

Dr. Linda Bogar: "Miracle? Is That *Really* His Name?"

Dr. Bogar earned her medical degree and completed surgical and cardiothoracic transplant fellowships at Temple University before completing cardiothoracic surgery residency at Thomas Jefferson University Hospital in Philadelphia. For more than fifteen years, Dr. Bogar has specialized in complex, high-risk cardiac surgery with a focus in heart and lung transplants, as well as mechanical circulatory support. Her résumé aside, she is a Christ-follower who has become a dear friend of our family.

■ ■ ■

When I was initially called for the ECMO evaluation and they told me the patient's name was Gary Miracle, I responded, "Miracle? Oh, come on, is that really his name?" I remember smiling and thinking, *Well, maybe that's a sign!*

Over Gary's 107 days in the hospital, his amputations, and many struggles, I would go see him as much as possible when I was at Advent. What always surprised me was that, on most days, he was very upbeat. I was also amazed at all the Bible verses and quotes his family had placed all over his room. There was always Christian music playing, and everyone who came to see him was so encouraging and positive. Of course, he had some down days when we would have to give him a little pep talk, but Gary was always gracious.

My interactions with his family and friends were always wonderful and pleasant. They were all so appreciative. We actually get quite a few people who don't treat the staff appropriately. So when people are consistently kind, it makes a huge difference and we take notice. That's one of the reasons I feel so blessed to know Gary and his family. A vivid memory for me was his dad—who rarely left his bedside—praying over Gary and telling him he knew he was going to pull through. Their bond was inspirational. Gary had an incredible network of support around him. As all doctors will attest, that dynamic is very important for a patient's survival and healing.

Yet, even with the amazing progress, Gary had some very difficult obstacles to overcome. When the amputations became inevitable, the timing was a real challenge. Surgeons like to wait until the last minute to allow as much tissue as possible to recover and be saved. The opportunity for prosthetics is far more viable when the joints for each limb are available and functioning. And rehab presents another challenge.

Throughout his stay, Gary became an inspiration to the entire staff because he proved that the ECMO device and connected technology can actually help someone survive and recover. But sadly, there are still a lot of people who don't pull through, even on the machine. Even with our amazing innovations today, there are no guarantees.

The day Gary left the hospital, the staff had a big celebration. We lined the halls while they wheeled him out, and everyone was happy for him and his family. Success stories like his are encouraging for all of us in the medical community.

As Gary and I have stayed in touch, he told me about the MercyMe song and video for "Say I Won't." When I watched it and heard the song, I was overwhelmed with emotion—such a powerful and amazing message. I showed the video to my entire family. The next time MercyMe came to Orlando, Gary invited me to the concert as a guest. I was glad to see that he was in such good health. After the concert, Gary introduced me to the band. For me, that was a dream come true. I thought about the full-circle moment when I walked into Gary's room while he was in a coma and hearing the band's music playing in his ear, to now getting to experience the music live with thousands of other people.

Before Gary left the hospital, he had promised me that he would come back to do anything he could to inspire patients and their families. By the time he returned to visit our ECMO unit, we had expanded from eight beds to thirty-two. He came up one day during rounds, greeted the staff, and gave an inspiring and emotional message. Gary closed by praying for everyone and expressing his gratitude for what we were doing. He also got in touch with our pastoral care team to offer any help he could provide in the future.

Lastly, I'm aware that Gary has referred to me as "the doctor who saved his life." I know he makes that statement because I agreed to place him on the ECMO machine. Although I did have to make that decision, I am *not* the *one* who saved his life. All the bedside nurses, doctors, surgeons, nurse practitioners, physician assistants, intensivists, kidney doctors, physical therapists, rehab specialists, and, of course, my surgical colleagues make up the *team* that saved him. The reality is that a large group of highly skilled professionals were involved in his care for all 107 days.

Yet, I do confess that having that kind of authority for such a life-and-death decision is a double-edged sword, both a blessing and a curse. Being in such a position is great in a case like Gary's where there is a happy ending, but during the pandemic, for example, that process almost broke me, just as it did many thousands of medical professionals. So many of us had to make those decisions every single day. Once we were fully immersed in the pandemic, ECMO became a very scarce resource. We had to carefully and critically evaluate each patient, to the point of triage, which was very difficult. People were calling from all over the country requesting to be transferred to our institution to get on ECMO. Too often, it became the only way to save people. The ultimate decision came down to us, the heart specialists and intensive care doctors in a collaborative discussion.

Over and over, I listened to people's stories from beginning to end, allowing them the opportunity to share, all the while knowing we did not have a bed for them. Having to say, "I'm very sorry, but I cannot help you" is horrible and devastating for everyone involved. The pandemic was tragic for all the people who suffered and died, their families, as well as all of us in the medical community. The toll was both personal and professional. Gary's ordeal happened right on the cusp of that season. Had he gotten sick during the pandemic, the outcome may have been quite different.

As a heart surgeon, I am placed in life-saving situations almost every day, especially for bypass surgeries and transplants. After a successful operation or procedure, I often have people say, "Thank you for saving my life." But my response is always the same, "Well, there was a team that worked together." For me personally, I always try to tell people that I'm not the ultimate one. God is simply working through me. That's why Gary's strong faith stood out to me. Every doctor has those patients we are always going to remember. Gary will forever be one of mine. His situation was so dire that I really did not think he was going to make it. But, by the grace of God, he is alive and well today, using his story to offer hope to a broken world.

Dad: The Other Gary Miracle

I'm a Junior, as in Gary Miracle Jr. My dad is the Senior. The other Gary Miracle. Yeah, evidently one just was not enough. My parents decided the world needed another.

I believe the person I saw transform the most through my ordeal was my dad. He was a strong Christian before, but walking through this with our family made him a different man, a more committed Christ-follower. The dad I have today is like nothing I had known before. Before he was great, but now, he's my hero.

■ ■ ■

At the time Gary initially got sick, I was fighting off something myself. So when we first got the call that he was admitted to the hospital, my wife went and I stayed home out of caution. We thought they would give him some fluids and meds, then he would be released in a few hours. But not long after my wife got there, she called, obviously emotional, and told me, "You better get up here. They're saying this could be the end." When you hear words like that completely out of nowhere, you are shocked; the moment is surreal. I immediately thought, *What in the world are they talking about?* My adrenaline kicked in. I forgot about how I felt and drove to the hospital as quickly as possible.

When I walked into Gary's room, not knowing what I would find, he was already hooked up to a bunch of machines and was totally out of it. Before long, a lot of other family and friends arrived. And, of course, everyone was in shock, with many questions about what had happened. As more folks arrived, the staff made us all go to the waiting area.

Once the decision was made to airlift Gary to another hospital, everything just got scarier and scarier. I had been praying, but now I started asking, "God, what in the world is happening here?!"

I know Gary has already told the helicopter story and how we later found out there was an accident somewhere and it had to be diverted. But in the moment, the questions of *what* and *why* were overwhelming. But I just knew we needed to trust what we believe, not just what we could see. Every detail would turn out to be part of God's timing. In the end, everything was going to work out exactly the way it should. In times like that, you know God says to trust Him, but it's hard when you feel like you're at the mercy of such dire circumstances. That first night was one of the most challenging times in my life.

Once we got to the hospital in Orlando, we found out Gary had coded on the table. After eleven minutes, a nurse detected a pulse. Soon after, Dr. Linda Bogar came out to the waiting room with an ICU doctor to meet us for the first time. I will never forget the care she gave our family. She sat down with us—so calm, polite, and genuinely concerned. The ICU doctor told us about Gary's 1.7 percent chance of survival and Dr. Bogar stated, "We've done all we can do." Then she gave us the only alternative, which was why she was there—the ECMO machine. She explained what it was and what it did. But she was very clear that Gary's situation would still be minute by minute.

Once the decision was made to put him on ECMO, they took him into surgery to hook up the machine. We were back in waiting mode again, which is a horrible place for a family to be. From that point, it was a long time before we left the hospital again. With Gary being so touch-and-go, leaving for any reason just wasn't worth the risk.

Once he was put into a room to be monitored, the staff never made us leave again. At any given time, there were between six to ten people in his room, often with more out in the waiting area. Everyone was gathered around, praying, and laying hands on him. I have never been more impressed with a group of people than I was with the nurses and doctors at the hospital. Those nurses had full control over that room to do whatever needed to be done at any given time with medication or treatment. To me, most of them looked like they were twelve years old when they were likely in their twenties, but every single one was incredibly skillful and professional.

While Dr. Bogar is certainly one of the most amazing people I've ever met in my life, Dr. Scott Silvestry constantly impressed me, too. Once, while Gary was on the ECMO machine, Silvestry stood in the doorway of the room, looking at the machines, and began to tell a nurse every number on every machine that he wanted adjusted. It was incredible to watch and hear. Of course, we had no idea what he was saying, but it was clear he was an expert in his field.

The moment I will never forget is when I walked into the hallway and Silvestry saw me. He walked over, put his hands on my shoulders, looked me in the eyes, and said, "Your son is going to live." For any parent, for a doctor to be that deliberate and assuring is a miracle. I can never thank Dr. Silvestry enough for his powerful and personal words.

As a father, I have never felt more useless in my life than in not being able to do *anything* to save my son. So I just prayed constantly. We *all* prayed constantly. And shed a lot of tears. There was so much emotion. Another moment that will forever remain with me was a time I was in the room alone with Gary. I was sitting in a chair at the foot of his bed when he opened his eyes for a moment and looked at me. It was as if he was trying to say, "Dad, do something. Help me. Save me." I got up, leaned over him, looked in his eyes, and took his hand. All I knew to say was, "I love you, son. I love you."

Any time Gary opened his eyes, we tried hard to fight back any tears so he would see us being positive. But as soon as he closed them again, the tears would flow. In that particular moment, I lost it. That's when you just have to remember that whether you are a father or a son, we both have the same loving, caring, ever-present Heavenly Father who is always in the room, watching over us all. When I felt helpless and had no idea what to do, I had to remind myself that *the* Father does.

During those first very fragile days, one of the pictures taken was of me standing by Gary's bed, leaning over him. Later on, Gary saw it and asked, "Dad, it looks you're talking to me. What were you saying?" I smiled and told him, "To keep fighting, just fight and fight and fight. . . . And how much I love you. That I was praying nonstop for you, and that we serve a great God who's going do great things for you."

Throughout those first days, we were always watching the machines. I can't tell you how many tubes and IVs were running into Gary's body. Every machine was beeping, giving us proof of life. But we also learned to watch the nurses. Any time one would do something different or get a look of concern on her face, we would start praying. Many times, we actually got to see the prayers answered. The timing of certain things happening and how it seemed anyone we needed was always in the right place at the right time was amazing. We've all heard stories about how God works miracles, but when you're actually living it in real time, your faith becomes stronger than ever.

I told a lot of people in those 107 days, "If someone doesn't believe in God, then they need to come spend a day with me in the hospital and watch how He is at work in my son's life." Every day, he was getting better, but every time something new came up, like dialysis or some other new procedure, we would pray.

When Gary was in the coma, not being able to communicate at all was so hard. Then when he woke up, couldn't speak, and had to mouth everything, my wife and I discovered we are not good at lip reading. We were having a hard time communicating with him and he would get really frustrated with us. Any time we saw him finally stop trying and close his eyes, we knew he was done, at least for the time being.

When he finally got his voice back and could speak, and we saw he was getting stronger, I realized that we had quit praying as much as we had in the life-or-death days. I thought, *Why are we doing this? We prayed for God to help him with so many things, and now that he's getting better, we're going to pray less? No! We still need to be praying and add praising!* That realization was important, because as time went by and we learned that Gary was going to start losing limbs, the reality hit us hard. Our prayers just had to move to different requests, not slow down.

As the weeks dragged on, a lot of the friends who had been so faithful had to get back to their normal lives, so there weren't as many people coming to visit as before. In those last weeks, it was just me and my wife and Gary's wife-at-the-time in his room. The three of us were there all 107 days, morning or night, doing anything we possibly could. We got to the point where the nurses would allow us to help clean Gary's wounds. We developed such a good rapport with them that we wanted to help them as much as we could. Any time a nurse would look at me and say, "You don't have to do this," or ask, "Why are you doing this?" I always answered, "He's my son. You never quit being a parent. I will do whatever I have to do to make sure he's comfortable."

Another strange occurrence was the story Gary has already told you about his dog, Bones. I was in the room, straightening and cleaning things up. I thought Gary was asleep when, all of a sudden, I heard him ask, "So, why didn't you want to tell me that Bones died?" Surprised at his question, I answered, "Well, son, there was no way I was ever going tell you that your dog died with everything you're going through." When I asked him how he knew, he told me the story of seeing Bones in his room and the realization that he had come to say goodbye. Just one of the countless things God did in that room.

As Gary began to make greater progress, I was impressed by his core strength. For anyone of any age, lying in bed for so long weakens you. The staff was telling him he was going to lose his legs but, as a part of the therapy regimen, they were also making him stand up. That was hard to watch. But when the time finally came for the amputation of his hands, I stayed with him until they took him back and then I went to the waiting room. I was there when he woke up and was one of the first to see him.

That was another time that was very hard to process. Standing there, looking at his stumps for the first time, I thought, *Here's my son, who I took to all his football and basketball games, watching him play from elementary to junior high to high school. Then in high school, watching him run track and become a state champion. And now he has nothing up to his elbows?* I often prayed, "God, what in the world are You doing? Why is this happening?" But as time went on, those prayers began to change to, "God, how are You going to use this?" I was concerned that Gary might give up at some point, just go home, and sit on the couch. But he was determined and accepted the new normal the best he could. We've watched him fight through so much, and he has maintained that same attitude to this day.

It's funny how our identities change over the years. I was just me for a long time. Then I was Linda's husband. Then I was Jennifer's dad. Then, Gary's dad. After both kids got married and were gone, I was back to me again. But as a result of all that has happened, once again, I'm Gary's dad. But, at every stage of life, my current identity has been a good thing and fine with me.

When Gary first came home, I went to the house every day to do whatever was needed, because that's when reality hit him. He wasn't sleeping or eating. He struggled with his therapy. The kids were amazing. They all pitched in. They didn't look at the situation like something was wrong with their dad. They just did everything they could to help him, especially Johana and Asher, the two oldest. It didn't matter what Asher was doing, every few minutes, he would stop and check on his dad. Gary had a great support system around him. We would talk almost every morning. I would take bagels over, help organize the mail, or take the kids to school, whatever was needed.

There were times we had to be loving but firm. For example, sometimes I had to say, "Let's do your exercises. You've sat there long enough." He went through a few prosthetic companies that were okay, but then one came along that has been a Godsend. They are absolutely the best in the world at what they do. They took Gary in, cared for him, loved him, and worked with him to get his arms and legs right. Throughout this ordeal, we have met some of the most amazing people in the world.

When Gary first started trying to walk on his prosthetics, he would say, "I don't think I can do this." Stan, who worked with the company, would tell him, "Gary, I'm going to have you walking by Friday! So just get *that* in your head. We're working and you're doing this!" He really pushed Gary, and Gary rose to the challenge. Eventually, he learned to drive again and then he also got back into coaching the boys' soccer and football teams. The parents seemed to appreciate that their sons had a coach they could see would never give up. There were built-in life lessons they could teach their kids, even just watching Gary out there on the field. While the boys were glad that their dad was coaching them, the hard part was they couldn't throw the football with him.

Today, Gary has six or seven guys in a tight circle who encourage, challenge, and support him. I've never met such a good group of guys as the ones in his corner. They're the best. Today, I often tell Gary, "I've been with you and heard your story so many times that if you ever have to cancel, I can fill in for you." We always laugh, because we both know that wouldn't be the same. When Gary walks out on the stage, he has preached a message before he ever opens his mouth. People see him and want to hear what he has to say.

Going back to what I said earlier about asking God how in the world He was going to use what happened to my son? Well, anytime I hear Gary speak to a crowd, I not only get my question answered, but I have the great privilege of watching God answer that prayer one more time. Today, Gary and I have a very unique, strong bond that will last forever.

I had the ultimate example of what *not* to do as a father from my own dad, who was mentally and physically abusive. I vowed that if I ever had a family I would never, ever put them through anything like what I experienced. When I trusted Christ as an adult, as Gary told you earlier, that made a very significant change in me. But then walking through what we did with Gary took me to a different level: I feel like I met God face to face. When you are standing in the middle of a room praying for a number on a device to change that nobody thinks can possibly change, and minutes later you watch the number go to what you asked for, that is *not* science. That is *not* medicine. That is *God*.

Joe: My Best Friend (After My Dog)

Joe and I met and bonded at the School of Ministry. Our friendship was one of the best things to come out of that season. Since then, we've always been close and bluntly honest with one another. But when I got sick, Joe stepped up like family. He is my dear brother in Christ that I know I can count on to be there in any circumstance. And I will do the same for him. Because of his commitment to stand with me, I wanted you to hear his unique perspective.

■ ■ ■

After being clean and sober for two years, I was leading a Celebrate Recovery group at our church. Some of the pastors and people there had encouraged me to apply for the School of Ministry. Even though I was reluctant and a bit skeptical, I decided to give it a try. The church accepted me, and I was in the next class of about twenty-five guys. Right away, I felt like a fish out of water. I had walked through Hell and back and was a little rough around the edges, as they say. I fit better in a recovery group or prison ministry than a Sunday school class or theology debate. But after a few classes, I met Gary and quickly saw he was much more like me. I could relate to him. When he told me that he felt out of place too, we had an immediate bond.

As our classes and assignments got rolling, we worked on projects together and called each other often for help. About a week before the mission trip to Colombia that we were scheduled to go on together, Gary told me, "Hey, I had this dream that I'm going to meet my daughter on this trip." Puzzled, I said, "But you don't have a daughter." He responded, "Right, but I'm going to adopt a girl down in Colombia." I was amazed to be an eyewitness when he actually did find his daughter, Johana.

After Gary and I managed to make it through the ministry school together, even though busy schedules often kept us from regularly hanging out, we always stayed in touch. We kept up with how we were both doing and consistently prayed for one another. We worked to stay connected through the ups and downs of life, having deep conversations and being accountable to one another. One thing Gary and I have always had is full-on transparent honesty with one another. We don't have to worry about making something sound pretty. We just tell it like it is, always maintaining grace and respect for each other.

The week that everything began for Gary, we had talked, and I knew he was sick. But with his age and health, I thought *Oh, it's just the flu*. I thought he'd be fine. None of us saw a threat to his life coming. Even when I found out that he went to the hospital in

Orlando, where I was, I assumed he would be given something and released. Had I had any idea the seriousness of his condition, I would have dropped everything and gone there immediately.

Once I found out what had occurred, the news was traumatic for me in two ways. One because of Gary's dilemma, but second, for several years, I had stayed away from hospitals. My first daughter was born with a lot of medical conditions. My wife and I spent eight months in the hospital with her before we were able to take her home. Several months later, she passed away. For me, hospitals had become a symbol of bad news, trauma, and death that triggered my grief and sadness. But I knew that I had to face the past and get over myself for Gary's sake.

As the days dragged on and he eventually came out of the coma, walking into Gary's room was difficult. That was one of the scariest sights I have ever seen. His condition made him look nearly inhuman. The first two feet of all his limbs were solid as a rock and a sickly brown color. Honestly, they looked like wood and, of course, his only movement at that time was trying to place his lips on a straw to drink.

As he began to slowly improve, every time I went to visit, I would bring him food. I was surprised when, one day, the staff told me, "Hey, Joe, you know you're the only person he'll eat for." That took my visits to an entirely different level of responsibility. I began to go every Sunday to stay with him. But every visit was still painful for a while.

Due to his need, our level of friendship went to a place most guys won't go. I would physically help him go to the bathroom. We had to leave pride, modesty, and any "bro boundaries" behind. That first month of my visits, we both just cried and held each other. If I'm being blunt, on an emotional level, at that time, Gary was defeated. Part of the problem was they had him on a lot of painkillers. The combination of drugs to alleviate pain, depression, and anxiety can make a person not want to live anymore. The fear I lived with was that one day I would walk into his room and, as his best friend, he was going to ask me to pull the plug or smother him with a pillow. I was terrified he was going to bring that up, but he never did.

People see and hear Gary now and say, "Wow! This guy is just a bundle of joy!" And that's true; he is *now*, but not then. There were Sundays when he would cry for three to four hours. There were times I massaged his back. I wanted to do anything to alleviate his suffering and comfort him—anything except help him die. More than anything, I wanted my best friend to live.

When Gary finally pulled through and his amputations were completed, we were excited. Several times, he and I talked about Job and how God took so much away, but then gave so much back. I felt like that was happening to Gary, but couldn't even imagine how it must feel.

When it was just Gary and the kids at his house, my wife and I would go over a few times a week to help out any way we could. I know both Gary and his wife-at-the-time went through the most traumatic experience of their lives during his illness and recovery. Those kinds of events change people. I knew that firsthand from losing my daughter. I ended up on pain pills, and eventually, addicted to heroin. I lost myself for nearly ten years. *Ten years*. So I get the traumatic experience of not wanting to live anymore. I get it completely.

But watching God rebuild Gary's life has been amazing. Everything started to come back together for him when he decided he wasn't going to let this crisis rule or ruin him. He made the intentional choice to make the most out of his new life. My wife and I did everything we could. Before Gary came home from the hospital, I went over and built wheelchair ramps over his steps.

A lot of people rallied around Gary through his ordeal, but I think the terrible thing for me was that even guys who had been in the ministry school with us never went to see him. Far too many people literally turned their backs on Gary. It was unbelievable and very sad. You'll never hear Gary bring that up. He will focus on who was there for him. But, as his best friend, feeling very protective, I struggled with knowing the people who just wrote him off because they would be uncomfortable around him or not know what to do or say.

On that subject, please let me say that when someone you care about has a personal crisis or tragedy, number one, don't make it about how you feel. Make it about the other person. Don't focus on the I's, as in, "I feel uncomfortable," or "I won't know what to say." Number two, ask yourself, *If that happened to me, what would I want and need from the people I know?* Then do that. And number three, if you don't have any idea what to do, for Heaven's sake, don't ignore the person. Give the ministry of presence, as in, "Hey, I'll be honest. I don't know what to say, but I'm here." Presence can mean much more than any well-wishes or Scripture quoting.

As I was with Gary Sunday after Sunday, I could tell his progress by his relationship with the nurses. At first, there were nurses he liked and ones he didn't. Some he didn't even want in the room. But as they began to decrease all his meds, especially the ones for pain, he was awake, alert, and interactive. Slowly, he began to be his positive self and talk more about what he was going to do when he got out of the hospital. Gary got more excited about the possibilities with prosthetics and how he might be able to walk one day. He was finding out about other people who had gone through similar situations. Over time, I saw Gary begin to have hope. I know when we lost our daughter, that's what I was searching for every day—hope. It's the one thing we all need to get through this broken world.

I'm blessed to have been able to watch Gary make it to where he is today. I don't think I could have handled losing him as my friend. But I'm awed and amazed to see where God is taking him. I love the guy. And I'm betting that, by now, you do too.

Jenna: The Gift of My Perfect Woman

I wanted to give Jenna her own space and place in this book to share some of her side of our story in understanding my journey to the present day. And I know for sure her words will minister to you.

■ ■ ■

Several months into our marriage, Gary and I found out about a young local man we didn't know who had been electrocuted, and it severely damaged his body. The jolt had stopped just short of killing him. We found out which hospital he was in and decided to visit. Why? Because we found out he had to have his leg amputated.

After we got to his room and introduced ourselves to him and his parents, Gary began to encourage him about his future. But, as he was sharing his heart, I was looking at the man's eyes, and felt like I knew deep down what he was already thinking: *I just lost my leg and half of my face is burned. Who's ever going to want me?*

That's where I have found my place in Gary's story. When he's done, I can step up, and confidently say to the amputee, "I don't see my husband's *lack* of hands and legs . . . his lack of *anything* . . . and I can tell you that someone will see *you* that same way someday."

One thing Gary and I have discovered is that everybody wants to know *his* story, but then they also want to know *our* story. Everyone perks up and wants to know how *we* happened. They want to ask us about it, but don't know how. They look at him and then look at me and think, *Why did you choose this life?* I'll answer the question, but first, here's some backstory . . .

Years ago, Gary and his ex-wife attended the same church as me and my ex-husband. Before that, we both homeschooled our kids for a while and we were in many of the same homeschool groups. Then, when his two boys who are on the spectrum started coming to my classroom for help, I got to know Asher well. Gary's kids and my kids have been in the same classes over the last few years. We were Facebook "friends," but there was never any real connection between me and Gary whatsoever.

When Gary got ill, I followed his journey through social media over those almost four months. I "watched" the whole thing unfold. I also noticed when it became obvious that he was separated and then divorced—which I also heard through the grapevine at school. At that point, I had been divorced from my ex-husband for about a year.

In 2021, I encountered a lot of health struggles with what has become known as "long COVID." The virus gave me tachycardia, which is a rapid and irregular heartrate. I couldn't walk and, for a while, I was in a wheelchair. I didn't know if I was ever going to get well and be normal again. For about six months, COVID took over my life. I spent a lot of time on the couch, trying to recover. The bottom line is, while we know I contracted the virus, the specifics of what it actually did to me are still a mystery. As of today, I am at about 80 percent.

With that information in mind, one of the most intriguing parts of our story involved my best friend who lives in Kansas. She's a pastor's wife, and we've been friends for more than twenty years. Yet never once in our relationship has she ever given me a "word from God," or anything like that.

But, when I was still very sick, she called and said, "Jenna, I had a dream that I feel like I need to share with you." Because this had never happened, she immediately had my full attention. She continued, "In my dream, you were at church again. You were healthy and involved in ministry again." With only those words, I was amazed and encouraged, but then she kept going. "But you were standing next to a guy who was a pastor, and he liked you. You were laughing a lot. He wanted to date you, but I didn't think he was your type. Yet you told me that you got really excited when he wanted to ask you out and that you would go for it. . . . But what was really weird, Jenna . . . is that the guy had no legs."

As a very ill single mom in my forties, I was amazed that she saw me healthy and laughing again. She saw me at church, in ministry, and ready to date. But when she said the guy had no legs, I said, "I only know of one guy who doesn't have legs, but I don't really know him at all."

That was my best friend's dream. As far as I was concerned, I would never get married again. I didn't even think I would date. I just didn't think it was a possibility. I was still so sick at the time, I couldn't really leave my house. Even when Gary did finally come into my world, I still was not in good health.

But our story began at a spring concert one of my children was involved in. Looking back today, I can see God in all of the details, even down to where I ended up sitting and where he was in the aisle in his wheelchair. I was there with my ex-husband, as we were working to coparent well. I saw Gary there and had a moment when I couldn't really identify the feelings I was having. I experienced butterflies, a crush, a schoolgirl sensation—whatever you want to call that. I felt excited and didn't really understand why. What I did know was this—I was attracted to Gary. Yet at the same time, it was very strange because I was on the same row as my ex-husband. That's just a weird dynamic.

I remember silently praying, *God, what is happening right now?* It was new for me to have any sort of feelings for another man, even though I had been divorced for a while. It was a lot to take in. But that night, nothing really happened. I remember walking past Gary and smiling. We acknowledged each other, but there was no other exchange. That was my first moment with Gary. Afterward, I didn't think much of it.

But about a week later, he sent me the now-infamous waving-hand emoji on Facebook. My initial response was to assume that Asher or Walter had gotten his phone and sent the message to be funny because I was their teacher. Surely a grown man wouldn't send me an emoji to try to talk to me for the first time? Not knowing if it was him or not, I just sent the "hi back" message.

I soon found out it was not one of the boys, but actually Gary. We began to message, and then traded phone numbers to talk. Gary is very charismatic and funny, so he had me laughing immediately. One thing I loved about him right away is that he's a man's man. He's a real guy's guy.

Even though our initial back-and-forth conversations were great, I was not yet at a place where dating was an option. I just didn't think I could. When Gary first began to approach me, I told myself, *Yeah, we can talk, but nothing will come of it. This is probably going to be pointless for you, buddy.* I was very upfront right away about my inability to date.

But Gary is so, well . . . he's Gary, so he pursued me. He was amazing to me, not fazed at all by my pushback. I was clearly interested in him but just felt, logistically, nothing could happen because of where I was with my life. I also had a lot of fear about men. But again, Gary being Gary, he just doesn't have any fear. He was so patient. The one thing I always say, and I think anybody who knows Gary would say about him: He's incredibly steady. *So* steady. He's consistent and doesn't get rocked by things most people would. I think that deeply affects his amazing ability to deal with whatever God brings him.

Now that I've given you some of my backstory, I'll answer the elephant-in-the-room question I promised I would—the biggest question people have for me. In our relationship, I didn't—and don't—even think about Gary not having hands and legs. That was not a factor for me, because I was more focused on my own limitations, struggles, and issues that would affect a relationship. I wasn't focused on anything Gary lacked, but more on what I still had to deal with to get healthy.

I don't want anybody to think I'm some kind of angel or saint for choosing Gary. I get that vibe when we're out and people see us. I've had people say, "Wow, you're amazing for choosing him." I wish I could have an hour to tell every single one of those people the real truth is that, yes, I did choose him, but he chose me, too! People don't know what I have gone through in my life—the very dark things that Gary walked through with me early on. But that is the very thing that made me fall in love with him. Those are the things that made me trust him and want to do life with him.

My response to Gary's condition may be because of what I've been through in my life. Or maybe it was from being sick for so long? Or maybe God just knew what Gary had to have? Or what I needed? But I don't look at my husband and see the big deal everyone else can't *not* see. That has never been a factor for me. I am just as attracted to Gary as I've been to any other guy for whom I've ever had any feelings.

Now, to be clear, while the physical issue doesn't affect me, I know how much it affects *him*. I know that he's reminded every day and how tough that is for him. But from where I'm standing, the way God gifted Gary and the way that I'm gifted, our marriage works because I'm a helper and a nurturer. I like to serve. I'm a caregiver. That's my nature and gifting. I have always been the one who did everything. I cooked. I cleaned. I homeschooled. That's just my role. So caring for Gary is not anything I wouldn't want to do anyway. My only challenge is emotional, when I see him struggling because he wants to do everything on his own. But even then, it just feels very normal to me.

I don't know fully what God wants to do with Gary and his story, but I'm a singer and I've led worship at Calvary Chapel, Fort Lauderdale, a 25,000-member congregation, so I understand a life committed to being on a stage, with all its attached expectations. I understand the responsibility of being in leadership and in the spotlight. I can relate to that aspect of Gary's calling now. I know the kind of personality and attitude a spouse needs to have to be okay with all that.

I watch Gary consistently choose life, and that causes me to choose life. The way Gary lives his life brought *me* back to life. I don't think I would be where I am physically if not for Gary pushing and encouraging me. He helps me not give in to the dark places that I can go sometimes. When I'm afraid that the tachycardia might make my heart stop at any moment, or I might eat something that triggers an anaphylactic reaction, Gary is an inspiration to me. When I'm tempted to give in to my fears, the way Gary lives his life now helps me get through. Gary is a what-you-see-is-what-you-get guy. That's who he is when it's just me and him.

And I want to emphasize this: "No more bad days" is not just a cool tagline to him. It's his lifestyle and attitude. Of course, we have bad days. He has bad days. But we're learning as we grow together that Jesus had the human side that we see in the Garden of Gethsemane. He cried out to God for help and strength in that dark moment. We're all going to have bad days. It's what you do and what we allow God to do in those bad days that ultimately matters. We have to make a choice. For Gary, that was answering, "Am I going to sit here and get addicted to pain pills and watch my life and my kids' lives go by and not do anything? Or am I going to get up and choose to live?"

As far as our kids blending, that has been a God thing, because they already knew each other. When we got together, my kids were eleven, nine, and seven years old. All the kids, except for Johana, were around the same ages. Gary's youngest, Henry, is a year older than my youngest, Joey. They were in the same first grade class together. Joey is obsessed with Henry. He wants to do anything Henry does and play whatever Henry is playing. Asher and Isabella, our oldest kids, have been in the same class since they were in the fourth grade. Those dynamics have helped our kids blend well together.

As for my relationship with Johana, for several years, I was a therapeutic-level foster mom for teenage girls and ran a group home. I worked in the world of adoption and foster parenting. From the start, I knew she and I might have a long, hard road as I tried to win her trust and acceptance. But at least I had the qualifications and experience to understand what she was walking through as she tried to accept our marriage. I told Gary many times, "I get it. It's hard. It's painful. But at the end of the day, I'm confident God knew that I would be her stepmom and I would be able to handle any emotional blows, along with all the things that she's going to feel. My hope is that one day she'll know that I'm safe, she can trust me, and I'm not going anywhere."

My past and what I've walked through prepared me for Gary, his life, and his children. I didn't walk into anything blindly. One time when we were still dating, Gary said, "I want to marry you," and then immediately started talking about his goals in life, about going out to speak and minister to people. Listening to him, my head started spinning, and I said, "Well, two things for me. One, I don't know if I can physically keep up with you. So second, with all that you feel God is calling you to do, I don't want to hinder you or get in your way." As I said previously, I understood the weight of all he was sharing. I understood he would need me to let him go while he does his ministry. I have all those points of reference too.

There will be times when the road is hard, and you have to know in those seasons that you are both called to it. Honestly, in that moment, I had more practical experience in what Gary was talking about than he did. I told him, "I hear you when you say what God wants to do with your life. I have to figure out if I fit into that." I had to wrestle with those thoughts and decisions. I'm not and wasn't going to be a fangirl. I knew what being his wife would mean if he was going to be a minister of the Gospel.

One of the things Gary has continued to say for us and about us is that our marriage is a ministry. As he and I were getting to know one another, I told him that one day I wanted to be back in full-time ministry. That's what I feel I'm called to do with my life, too. While I don't always know what that looks like, I know the calling is there. A few months into our marriage, after we had worked through some major bumps that he shared with you, I was spending time in the Word and got to 1 Peter 4:10–11. Here it is:

> God has given each of you a gift from his great variety of spiritual gifts. Use them well to serve one another. Do you have the gift of speaking? Then speak as though God himself were speaking through you. Do you have the gift of helping others? Do it with all the strength and energy that God supplies. Then everything you do will bring glory to God through Jesus Christ. All glory and power to him forever and ever! Amen.

Goosebumps. I went straight to Gary, read the passage to him, and said, "This is us! This is it! 'Each of you' is us. We are to use our gifts well to serve one another. You have the gift of speaking and I have the gift of helping others. So then we serve together and use our gifts with all the strength and energy that God supplies to bring glory to Him. When you speak, it is just natural and God-given. You don't ever have to think about it. You just always have to focus on making sure your heart is positioned to give God glory, because He gave you this gift. And then I will follow you anywhere. I'm ready to put your legs on. I'm ready to talk to whoever I need to talk to. I'm just ready to be there. I want to help whoever God brings across our path and do what they need to help them. I'm excited for that."

But we know Satan hates marriage, because God created and ordained it—especially those that are submitted to God. When Gary and I got married, we didn't know what we didn't know. We thought we were healed. We thought we had done the work. We thought we were okay. But the next part of our sanctification was going to happen within our marriage. That's why we had such a rude awakening. God had more surgery to do on us, separately and together.

That's why Gary and I have agreed that if we're going to be honest in ministering to others, if we're going to inspire people and allow Him to use our story for His glory, we need to be transparent about the hard things, too. Everybody wants to talk about the restoration. There are highs *and* lows, but much of life is lived in the middle place, so we have to talk about the middle stuff too. Think about the Book of Psalms. One of the reasons David's songs minister to us is that he sings praises at the beginning of a chapter and then cries out to God for answers in frustration and angst in the middle—often ending on a note of trust in God despite the hardship he faces. That's why I know our story can give so many people hope.

As I mentioned before, I'm insanely attracted to Gary—like, stupidly attracted to him. Sometimes I hate how attracted I am, because it makes me vulnerable. I see my husband as whole. I feel blessed to have him. I don't *have to* be in a relationship with Gary. I *get to* be in a relationship with Gary. In so many ways, our marriage is no different than anyone else's.

Gary told me that when I said "hi back" to him, he had a moment when he thought, *I know I'm going to marry you*. Through a series of events happening all around us, he felt like he knew. Obviously, I didn't know right away. But the way that Gary was handling my heart, my children, and all the dynamics in my life, I soon knew that I was falling in love with him. I began to feel like what was happening between us was redemptive, like God was giving me back so much of what I had lost. Just like Gary quotes Job 1:21—the Lord gives and takes away, but blessed be the name of the Lord.

Neither of us was interested in dating just to date, and as we began to talk about marriage, we found we were of the same mind. We also got extremely honest about our wants, needs, and deal-breakers: "Here's my line in the sand." Every time I presented one of those, Gary's response made me feel safer and more secure with him. As the days went on, I was trying to weigh all the heavy issues I could regarding what it would mean to be married to Gary. I eventually came to the conclusion that I could trust my life and my children's lives to him.

I was very protective of my children. I wouldn't talk or Face-Time with Gary until they were in bed. For their sakes, I was treading very lightly. The icing on the cake became the reality of us doing ministry together and our marriage being a ministry. That was my heart. I could feel God leading every moment and all the doors opening.

It was really no surprise that Gary had this huge, grand moment prepared for his proposal. He had a beautiful song cued up and ready for when we walked into the house. The moment was just us in private and wasn't a big show. That's what I wanted. Even in that moment, I felt so loved and cared for by Gary because he did what I needed, not what he wanted. He made it so easy to say yes. The entire proposal was perfect. Little did I know, he also had a camera going to capture the entire moment to share with family and friends. And, just as he told you, he proposed at night and the next day we got married.

Gary and I have had to admit that we don't know exactly what God is going to do or specifically where we're headed, but while keeping our marriage sacred, we both know we need to be transparent about the journey. We believe God wants to use us together to help people find truth and to understand how redeeming life can be in Him. There are a lot of hard days for us, so we know we must constantly allow God to hold our hands through it.

I have one last story to encourage any women, whether single, divorced, or widowed, who may have lost hope in finding someone. When I heard Gabby Barrett's song "The Good Ones," I was taken with the lyrics and the message. After my divorce but well before I met Gary, I woke up in the middle of the night with that song on my mind. The next morning, I sensed the voice of God telling me, "I have this for you, Jenna. I have this man for you." I knew that what I heard was beyond my own wishful thinking and hopes for the future. It came in the same way God had spoken to me in the past.

I was not in a place to fully accept the word right then. I even thought, *No, this is not for me*. I wasn't trying to live in denial, but just realistically looking at my circumstances.

I'm so grateful that, once again, I was wrong and God was *so* right. So, if you feel the way I felt, take heart, because God can definitely bring beauty from ashes. He did that for me, and He can do the same for you.